If you are looking for a practical, science-based guide to leading change—then you must read this book! It is the ultimate guide for driving real progress.

—Dr Amantha Imber, Head Inventiologist of Inventium, Innovation Scientist and best-selling author of *The Creativity Formula*

~

This book explodes the myths of motivation and maps a world of willing, voluntary and enthusiastic work.

—Dan Gregory, Behavioural Strategist and Director of The Impossible Institute and *Gruen Planet* panellist

~

The Game Changer *busts futile myths in motivational folklore, and takes an evidence-based approach to the (art and) science of driving change. You will benefit greatly from the insights and design intent evident in this cheekily heretical and iconoclastic game changer!*

—Anders Sörman-Nilsson, Futurist and Founder of Thinque and author of *Digilogue*

~

This is an extraordinary book—a complete game changer for motivation and influence.

—Matt Church, best-selling author of *Thought Leaders* and *Amplifiers*, and Founder of Thought Leaders Global

the CHANGER GAME

the CHANGER GAME

How to use the science of motivation with the power of game design to shift behaviour, shape culture and make clever happen

DR JASON FOX

WILEY

First published in 2014 by John Wiley & Sons Australia, Ltd
42 McDougall St, Milton Qld 4064

Office also in Melbourne

Typeset in Weidemann Std 10/12.5 pt

© Dr Jason Fox

The moral rights of the author have been asserted

National Library of Australia Cataloguing-in-Publication data:

Author:	Fox, Jason, 1983- author.
Title:	The Game Changer: how to use the science of motivation with the power of game design to shift behaviour, shape culture and make clever happen/Dr Jason Fox.
ISBN:	9780730307648 (pbk)
	9780730307662 (ebook)
Notes:	Includes index.
Subjects:	Motivation (Psychology).
	Management.
	Games.
	Leadership.
	Employee motivation.
	Creative ability in business.
	Creative thinking.
	Corporate culture.
Dewey Number:	650.1

Cover design by Xou Creative, www.xou.com.au

All illustrations by Dr Jason Fox

10 9 8 7 6 5 4 3 2 1

Disclaimer

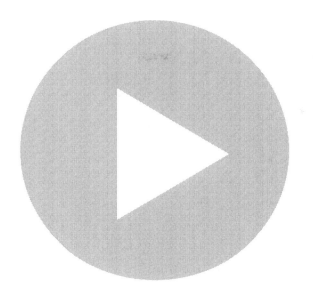

Game Changer

noun: a newly introduced element or factor that changes an
existing situation or activity in a significant way

CONTENTS

ABOUT THE AUTHOR

Dr Jason Fox is a global authority on motivation strategy and design, and he's on an epic quest to liberate the world from poorly designed work.

After sneaking into the Ivory Towers of academia and levelling up with a PhD in record time, Jason now works with forward-thinking business leaders, showing them how to use the best elements of motivation science and game design to influence behaviour, drive progress and make clever happen.

He has advised on motivation strategy, change management and good gamification design to a range of organisations — from multinational companies like PepsiCo, Gartner and Toyota; to the big banks, universities, mining, telecommunication and pharmaceutical companies; right through to grassroots educational organisations and savvy startups.

Jason lives in Melbourne, Australia, the hipster capital of beards and good coffee. When not gallivanting around the world speaking at events (as the science-based alternative to the fist-pumping rah-rah motivational corporate speakers) or immersed in game-changing work with clients, Jason enjoys partaking in extreme sports like reading, coffee snobbery and *fruit ninja*.

Learn more at www.drjasonfox.com.

ACKNOWLEDGEMENTS

Writing a book is bloody hard work. I'd love to pretend that I gamed my own motivation, and that the whole thing was double rainbows, unicorns and cupcakes — but the fact is this book would not have been possible without the support of some truly inspiring people. The type of folk you feel lucky to have met and have in your life. The people that keep you real, and actively contribute to your quest.

For me, this adventure was kickstarted by my good mates and thought leaders Matt Church, Darren Hill and Peter Cook. They've all published brilliant books with Wiley, and all worked to sneak me in the back door to speak to the right people (and helped to keep me on track). You guys are legendary.

Those right people at Wiley were Kristen, Elizabeth and Keira — all super brilliant. Kristen was enthusiastic and supportive of the concept right from the start. Thank you for helping me to keep the book funky and fresh. And Elizabeth, thank you for being so kind and patient during those prolonged bouts of perfectionism.

This book wouldn't be the book it is without the help of a professional editor. I've got to give a big thanks to Jem Bates, who has completely revolutionised my perceptions of the editing process. His thorough, empathetic and constructive approach has made this a much better book.

I must also give thanks for some of the support I had on the sidelines. Jen Storey, your editing help early in the game got me across the line a number of times — thanks for contributing your wit and helping to dig me out of a few ruts. And Russel Remigio, my 'Wonderuss' assistant — thank you for embarking upon the obscure research quests that contributed to this book (and curtailing the entropy in my absence).

Of course there's also the family and friends one neglects as they conquer a project like this. Thanks guys for still liking me, even as I become ever more obscure.

And then there are the clients I've had the honour of working with. You've all helped shape the ideas in this book, and I'm mighty grateful.

But the biggest thanks of all must go to my gorgeous wife, Kim Lam (aka 'Dangerlam'). This book would not be possible without her. Kim has supported me throughout it all. Even when I was away working with clients overseas, and writing this book instead of cooking dinner, or bringing the laptop to restaurants to work on this through dinner, Kim has been ridiculously supportive of this project. Thank you darling, for the light and the laughter you bring to my every day. I love you to bits.

Ah! And thanks to you too. For being the type that reads the acknowledgements, and of course for supporting this book. I'm already liking the cut of your jib. Hat tips to your magnificence! We're going to get along mighty fine...

THE BIG QUESTION: HOW DO YOU MOTIVATE PEOPLE TO DO <u>GREAT</u> WORK?

'You can do it!' roars the motivational speaker. 'All you need to do is BELIEVE in your ability to ACHIEVE, and you will SUCCEED! Repeat after me: conceive, believe, achieve. Conceive, believe, achieve. Conceive, believe, achieve...' Fist-pumps abound.

Except...you know motivation doesn't work like that. You can inspire people—and be inspired—all you like. But unless you change the game, nothing changes. Inspiration is like milk: it expires. And what you're left with is the work required to make your goals and ideas happen.

'So let's just offer a bonus reward', says the manager, eager to see change happen. 'If we offer a bonus, people will do it.'

And sure, you can change the game by adding in a reward. But, you'll be shifting the motivational dynamics and potentially hobbling creativity and collaboration in the process. People might get so focused on the reward that they take shortcuts that undermine the whole process.

Motivation is a tricky thing. And work is changing.

To stay ahead of the game, and to make great things happen, we need to change the way we design our projects and processes so we can sustain and amplify the desire, or motivation, to do great things.

That's what this book will show you—how to change the game so that work and change become inherently motivating.

'What's this talk of games?' I hear you ask. Well, we'll unpack that in glorious detail in chapter 6. But for now let's roll with this: games are the interplay between goals, rules and feedback. A good game is a goal-driven, challenge-intense and feedback-rich experience geared towards progress. These three components correlate to our modern understanding of intrinsic, non-contingent motivation—purpose, mastery and autonomy (more on this in chapter 3).

It so happens that you could take the definition of a game and apply it to nearly any meaningful project or process at work. All projects and work consist of goals, rules and feedback. But sometimes the goal is misaligned, the rules don't work or the feedback loops get out of whack. By changing the game, we can shift motivation and unlock progress.

*It's not you. It's **it**.*

For too long, many of us have been led to believe we need *more* motivation. If we don't have the motivation to work towards an important goal, or to drive ourselves to succeed, or to think differently, we feel that there must be something wrong with us. That we are somehow lazy or have a poor attitude.

But there's nothing wrong with us; we simply cannot function at high levels of motivation in all things at all times. Fact. But what we *can* do is craft the games that keep us motivated and aligned to progress the work that matters.

This book will show you how to drive motivation, not just through inspiration, or remuneration, but by fixing the structure of your goals, projects and work.

*It's not **dependent** upon you either.*

If you're leading a team, you'll know that it's hard work carrying the motivation torch all the time. You can give your rousing speeches, and you can put on a big event to kick off the year, and maintain a state of perpetual optimism—but what happens when you're not around? Does everything collapse into monotonous, repetitive automation?

This book will show you how to craft the games that will sustain the motivation of others and how to get your team doing great things, even when you're not around.

Old-school tools make for new-school fools.

We've all endured presentations on SMART (specific, measurable, achievable, relevant and time based) goal setting. We've all heard sage adages like 'Whether you think you can or you can't, you're right'. And many of us have experienced organisations that suffer from perpetual shiny-new-process syndrome, where there's a new fad program each year: 'Neurolinguistic programming? Oh yeah, we did that five years ago. Design thinking? Yep, we did that too. What's next?'

But we can do better than that.

Much of what we have traditionally learned about managing motivation came from the factory era, when the focus was on productivity, efficiency and performance. While this is still relevant for today's work, what's emerging, and what the old tools often fail to address, is the need for motivational dynamics that inspire and support creativity, collaboration and agility. These are the core ingredients for innovation, change and progress.

This book will show you how to use the right game elements to create the motivation needed to drive progress.

There's always a game at play.

This book isn't called *The Game Changer* simply because it's a catchy title. We're going to unpack some of the sophisticated design elements of games, combine them with what we know from the science of motivation, and apply these new rules to every project and process challenge at work.

Right now, more than half a billion people (the vast majority of whom are adult men and women) spend more than 5 billion hours each week playing online video games with a level of focused engagement that we just do not see at work. There's a heap of savvy that we can take from this phenomenon to apply to the game at play.

This is because there's always a game at play. And you, the game changer, must learn the rules—so that you can tweak, bend, break or remake them to get the results you want.

Abandon all hope. And fluff.

And so maybe this is all a bit too confronting. If you're searching for warm fuzzies and feel-good fluff, this probably isn't the book for you.

The world of motivational books is rife with inspiration and stories of hope. Inspiration is fine, as it's the precursor to aspiration and motivation. But hope? That's nice, but you don't need hope. Hope is only helpful when you're hope*less*.

And you're not hopeless. You have the ability to make dramatic changes to the way you and the people around you progress to meaningful goals through work that matters.

So, let's abandon all hope and fluff. This book will give you the science to make game-changing work a reality.

Let's move beyond inspiration and the cult of success.

Now that we've got hope out of the way, let's rethink the cult of success. This book is going to encourage you to fail. The path to innovation and any meaningful growth, change and improvement is non-linear and fraught with failure.

This is not a new thing. It is estimated that gamers spend 80 per cent of their time failing, and Einstein reckons 'play is the highest form of research'.

Success is simply *a failure to fail.*

If that doesn't work for you, think of it like this: in science there is no such thing as failure, only disproven hypotheses. Thomas Edison, the famous and very prolific innovator, probably had this figured out best. He was quoted to have said, 'I have not failed — I've just found 10 000 ways that won't work'. Edison made a distinction between personal failure and failures in a particular *methodology.* And that's something this book will help you understand.

So, we can either retreat and cook up perfect new visions, goals and plans (note: there's no such thing), or we can tackle changes iteratively, conducting micro-experiments and launching progress-making games where it's safe (and smart) to fail fast.

If you're a perfectionist, I'm going to show you how to become a progressionist. And, if you're worried about failure, I'm going to show you how to reframe failure and make it work for *progress.*

For you, the game changer, there are only good games and games *yet to be made better.*

Culture is not the target.

Let's remember what we're doing here. This is about shifting what influences human behaviour. You've heard people talk about culture. You can't see it, and you can't touch it—but you can *feel* it, and you know it's there. And you know it underpins all the results you get, good or bad.

But culture is something you can't tackle directly. So how do you change culture?

You use science, and you start with the right motivation design (see figure 0.1).

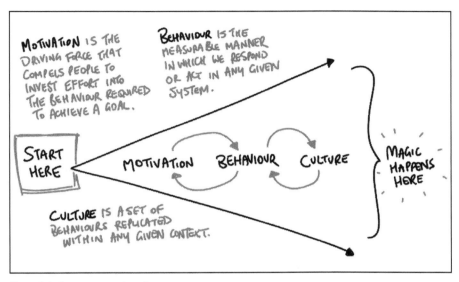

Figure 0.1: the precursors to culture

This book—particularly chapter 8—will show you how you can create the artefacts and implement the rituals that will begin the process of changing behaviour that, in turn, will shift the culture of your organisation or team.

It all starts with, and comes back to, motivation strategy and design.

Motivation is backwards—but you can set it right.

We're going to change things here, you and I. But not everything I share with you is going to work. There's no 'one-size-fits-all' magic silver bullet—but you know that.

And there are no hidden motivational secrets either, but there's a whole heap of savvy from the world of game design that just hasn't been translated clearly into real-world practice (until now).

But if we're going to make this work, there are three principles behind changing the game:

1. **Motivation is part of a bigger, complex system.** To shift motivation we tweak the system, working from the outside in (rather than from the inside out, as most prescribe).

2. **Change is the only constant.** Our game-changing work needs to be fluid, adaptive and iterative. We place more emphasis on proximal process than distant goals.

3. **Progress is the only thing that matters.** Perfection, productivity, efficiency — all of these are secondary. If in doubt, always ask, 'Are we making progress happen?'

There we go, easy! Ha, maybe not. But, let's navigate through the uncharted waters of motivation design and see where we end up.

But where are my 'top ten tips'?

You won't be finding a simple set of instructions to follow mindlessly that'll make motivation, progress and change work. Not in this book.

There are far too many books out there dumbing motivation down to the point where people stop thinking about what they're doing. And that's the problem — we don't tackle motivation with the strategy and design required to make it work. Instead, we simple look to 'gold standards' that are old by the time they're recognised as gold. And then when we've got a supposed gold standard, we try to force-fit what works in one context into another.

Nah, we're not doing that here. Leadership author David Marquet says: 'If you want people to think, give them intent — not instruction'.

My intent with this book is to help you think about motivation, progress and change with more strategy and design. This book largely unpacks an *approach* you can take to solve any motivation challenge at work, to shift behaviour, shape culture and make clever happen.

The game changer is that newly introduced element that makes a significant difference to the game in play.

Sometimes I refer to the game changer as 'you, the game changer'. In fact, there's a whole chapter called that.

But it's not really about you or me. Just as it's rather lame for people to call themselves entrepreneurs on their business cards, game changers don't call themselves game changers. They're just people who tinker with the structures that influence motivation and shift behaviour.

A game changer is really a person who actively seeks, experiments with and implements new elements that lead to significant positive change. This might be the introduction of a competitive game element, heightened progress feedback, a narrative layer.

Speaking of which, you might be tempted to flick ahead to the juicy bits in chapters 7 and 8. Please don't—not just yet. There are a few things we need to get working first in order to get the motivation strategy right, and to mitigate some of the shadow effects inherent within every motivation element. Otherwise we may end up stuck in the same cycle of short-sighted motivational 'tips and tricks' many managers and leaders succumb to.

So, stick around as we embark upon an epic quest to find the game changer and liberate the world from poorly designed work.

HOW TO USE THIS BOOK

Treat it like an ace up your sleeve the next time you want to tackle any motivation, behaviour or culture change challenge.

This book is divided into three main parts:

Part I: The motivation savvy-up

Here we cut through the motivational folklore and conventional managerial wisdom to establish what really works to build and sustain motivation through change.

Chapter 1: A most alluring motivational folklore

This chapter will help you to rid the world of the Cult of Success and to start embracing the structures that work to amplify the motivation you've already got.

Chapter 2: An imperative for change

A book called *The Game Changer* talking about change? Well I never! But fret not, we're not focusing too much on 'the need for change' here. I'm sure you get that already. Instead, we get pragmatic about what it takes to make change happen in organisations, and what we're up against.

Chapter 3: And yet... the big motivation gap

All progress, growth and change lives in the gap between where we are and where we want things to be. Many have tried to gloss over the fact that success takes work. Lots of work. And yet the key to all of this is making the work bit *work*.

Part II: Getting your game on

Here we unpack the power of progress and what games are, why they complement the science of motivation so well, and how incredibly powerful game design can be in influencing real-world behaviour and change.

Chapter 4: The root of all game-changing hacks

Here I reveal the simplest and most effective way to generate more motivation in any situation—it forms the basis of all game-changing hacks.

Chapter 5: Get your head into the game

Change has been covered, and now what's this talk of games? Well, they just happen to hold the secret to blissful productivity, amplified authenticity, urgent optimism and epic meaning. They're worth a good look—because a lot that works in the world of game design can be applied to drive progress in the real world.

If you're a rogue scholar already well versed in the classic and contemporary elements of motivation science, this chapter will help you get your head into the game (so you can change it and play a better game).

Chapter 6: A model game changer

And now you are ready for the *Game Changer* model—an alchemy of motivation science and game design.

Part III: Changing the game

Having savvied up on the science of motivation and the power of game design, now we roll up our sleeves and get into the game-changing elements that shift behaviour and shape culture.

Chapter 7: Lift your game

This chapter will help you smash through self-sabotage and use game design to hack your own motivation. If you're playing the lone wolf, and want to hack your own motivation, you'll love this chapter.

Chapter 8: Change the game

And now we cast our eye over the wider team and organisation, crafting rituals and structures to influence motivation, shift behaviour and shape culture. If you're leading teams and influencing change within organisations, this chapter will be like nirvana.

Chapter 9: You, the game changer

From hacking your own motivation, to that of your team, to shaping the very culture of your organisation — you're on a hero's journey here.

Righto, so let's do this thing. First up, we've got some *unlearning* to do. Get your pen ready...

PART I ▶

THE MOTIVATION SAVVY-UP

A MOST ALLURING
MOTIVATIONAL FOLKLORE

Too many organisations still operate from assumptions about human potential and individual performance that are outdated, unexamined, and rooted more in folklore than in science.

— Daniel Pink

Before we get too far ahead of ourselves, let's make sure we embark upon this quest cleansed of the many misconceptions that plague motivation. The land of motivation is rife with delightful stories and well-intended advice. But much of what we know, and a lot of what makes up conventional wisdom in this space, is warped.

Now don't get me wrong, I'm not about to say that Everything You Know About Motivation Is Wrong (that comes later). But most of us have a warped sense of how motivation works. The science gets distorted and bent out of shape.

Stuff gets warped

This happens in science all the time. Jorge Cham, the creator of PhD Comics (brilliant), once wrote a comic on 'The Science News Cycle'. (I get a lot of my research from comics, by the way, #credibilityftw.) It went something like this:

> Scientists will discover a weak correlation between A and B, assuming C under D conditions. The university PR office will then post something for immediate release: 'Scientists Find Potential Link Between A and B (under certain conditions)'. News organisations will pick it up and publish, 'A causes B, say scientists', which will then be read by The Internets and turned into 'A Causes B — ALL THE TIME!' Which will then be picked up by TV shows that run stories like 'A...A Killer Among Us??' All of this eventually leads to your grandma getting all weird about A.

You may have heard about the Yale Goal Study — a perfect example of warped science.

In 1953 a team of researchers interviewed Yale's graduating year, asking them if they had written down specific goals that they wanted to achieve in their career and life. Only 3 per cent of the students had.

Twenty years later the researchers tracked down the same cohort and discovered that the 3 per cent of graduates who had written down specific goals all that while ago, well, they had accumulated more personal wealth than the other 97 per cent of their cohort. Combined.

It's a great story, frequently cited in self-help books and seminars to illustrate the power of goal setting. And back when I was a young researcher in motivation science and goal setting it was a story I loved to share with my students.

Except there's just one small problem. Richard Wiseman, a scientist renowned for dispelling myths, points out: 'As far as anyone can tell, the [Yale Goal] experiment *never actually took place'*.

No one could produce any evidence that the research had ever been conducted, prompting journalist Lawrence Tabuk to publish an article in *Fast Company* in 2007 titled, 'If Your Goal is Success, Don't Consult the Gurus'. The motivational speakers and gurus, myself included, had been happy to share this story without checking the facts.

How did we become so deluded?

Because, like all good myths, there are seeds of truth to it.

Yes, goal setting *is* more powerful when it is written down, and yes, it *is* more effective when it is framed in specific, rather than vague, terms. There are plenty of studies to support this. But more effective for what?

Productivity? Yes, maybe; a lot of research into goal setting comes from the factories and shows it works well for formulaic tasks with predictable outcomes over a set period of time, as well as other tasks that require narrow focus.

But for creative aspiration, innovation and change? Maybe not; often, specific goal setting can lead to narrow thinking, hobbled creativity and purpose-defeating shortcuts. We'll talk about this more in chapter 3.

'But no one told the bumblebee!'

I once heard a motivational speaker attempt to instil a positive attitude with this story: 'Did you know that according to the laws of aerodynamics the bumblebee can't fly? But guess what — no one told the bumblebee ... People are going to tell you that you can't fly either. Ignore them, and let your wings shine!'

I can't stand warped fluff like that. And nor should you.

A scientist would simply explain that this assumes small amplitude oscillations without flow separation, ignoring the effect of dynamic stall, which causes an airflow separation inducing a large vortex above the wing. This vortex briefly produces several times the lift of the aerofoil in regular flight. The bumblebee flies because its wings encounter dynamic stall on every down stroke. And when you consider that bees beat their wings approximately 200 times a second, it's no wonder they can fly. Bam. That's science.

Positive thinking and the danger of belief

'Just believe in yourself.' It's a great piece of advice that can easily get warped out of proportion, along with 'You need to dream big!'

The trouble with this fluff is that it's a bunch of meaningless words that are so much easier to say than to actually do. Arousing people by telling them of the potential you see in them serves only to widen the gap of discontent between where they are and where they think they should be. This discontent can be constructive, but if there are no structures to bridge this gap, all you are left with is a more acute sense of discontent.

Imagine this: Little Johnny is told he can achieve anything he wants to — all he needs to do is believe. And he really does believe it! He is inspired! He's visualising his success, and keeping himself motivated with positive affirmations. Every negative thought is countered with a positive one.

Except... as time goes on, the evidence he is collecting does not support this new belief in what can be achieved. There's a big mismatch. And positive thinking just reinforces the negative thoughts that trigger it. Eventually, the rational part of Johnny's brain wins, and he gives up pursuing his goal. His sense of self-belief collapses, and his enthusiasm for aspiration and pursuit of worthy projects is *less* than it was before.

And understandably so. Big goals, blind optimism and unfounded self-belief can lead to apathy and depression. And depression is a bitch.

But there is a school of thought that depression is a natural mechanism to keep our goals in check. Randolph Nesse, a professor of evolutionary medicine at the University of Michigan, suggests that depression may be an adaptive mechanism to protect us from falling victim to blind optimism. It's to our evolutionary advantage to avoid wasting energy on goals that we can't realistically achieve. And so when we are faced with no clear way to make progress, depression kicks in, triggering a lower state of energy.

Modern society encourages us to aspire to fame, glory and fortune. If these goals are beyond us or literally unattainable, we can become disenchanted. Nesse argues that this could be a contributing factor to the depression epidemic in countries like the United States.

Philosopher Alain de Botton also suggests that our pursuit of higher 'status' is the source of much anxiety and angst in modern society. 'Anxiety is the handmaiden of contemporary ambition', he argues. Many people avoid setting big, well-structured goals for fear of what a failure to achieve them might mean in their social ecology, at work or at home:

> The attentions of others matter to us because we are afflicted by a congenital uncertainty as to our own value, as a result of which affliction we tend to allow others' appraisals to play a determining role in how we see ourselves. Our sense of identity is held captive by the judgements of those we live among.

Thus the easiest way to avoid judgement is to avoid placing yourself in situations in which you are judged. To not set goals, and to not play games.

Obviously, this is not good for progress.

So how do we generate and sustain the motivation to achieve big dreams and audacious goals (without falling into the traps and pitfalls along the way)?

Getting strategic with optimism

As we know, blind optimism — the automatic 'yes' to any idea — can be dangerous. And of course, pessimism — the automatic 'no' to any idea — also sucks.

What we need to be is *sceptically* optimistic. This is way more strategic. Where your default optimists and pessimists prejudge things to be positive or negative, a sceptical optimist will reserve judgement until they have the evidence (all the while maintaining an optimistic outlook).

'But without prejudging things as right or wrong, where do we get our sense of belief from?' I hear you ask.

'The evidence!' I say. You build optimism and literally make believe by doing the work that contributes to progress.

But if we don't have evidence to start with ... hmm, this is the tricky predicament. Like the chicken and the egg, which comes first, the belief or the evidence?

This is where we need to suspend disbelief

Suspended disbelief was a term coined in 1817 by the philosopher and poet Samuel Coleridge. It's what we usually experience when we're reading a good book, or immersed in a movie. Emotions and crazy stuff seems real in the moment, and the combination of the images you see and the sounds you hear can trigger emotional and physiological reactions—even though the rational part of your mind knows it's not real.

This is why we work with useful hypotheses. In science, nothing is true or untrue—there are merely hypotheses waiting to be tested. So, in essence it's not just disbelief that needs suspending; it's belief too.

Peter Cook, a good friend of mine and the author of *The New Rules of Management*, has a good perspective on this. Before becoming a global business thought leader, Pete was a physicist. This has grounded him with pragmatic insight into how theories work:

> The problem is that just about every theory we've ever had to explain the universe, while it may have been useful, has turned out to be wrong. The Earth was flat ... then it was round. It was at the centre of the solar system ... until it wasn't. Then Newton described how things moved ... until Einstein came along and explained why he was wrong. And recently some pretty smart people have worked out how Einstein was wrong too.
>
> If history is anything to go by, all the current theories will be superseded by more useful theories that better describe the universe at some time in the future.
>
> I think our beliefs are similar. None of them are true. If all these Nobel-winning physicists, some of the smartest people in history, were wrong about the most objective discipline we have, isn't it a bit arrogant, even ludicrous, for me to think that my beliefs about anything, but particularly about myself, are true?

Pete suggests a better question to ask is 'Are my beliefs *useful*?'

And I couldn't agree more. It makes sense to delude yourself with positive beliefs about your ability to achieve things before you have the evidence. Just as long as you know that it is a delusion, and don't go jumping off cliffs believing you can fly.

If you want to progress change within reason, know that positive delusions like this can't be sustained without the accumulation of *evidence* to support it.

And there's no doubt you're going to encounter some blind optimism and a lot of pessimism. People will have prejudged what's possible, and what's not. The only way to really find out is to collect evidence, by conducting experiments and play-testing new ideas.

Rather than relying on blind hope or artificially inflated self-belief, and rather than simply waiting until evidence has been collected by others, the best way to stay motivated and progress through game-changing work is to be strategically optimistic, conducting behavioural experiments while operating with suspended disbelief.

It's really the only way forward.

Overcoming the cult of success

'Because what we need to do is upgrade our _____? Come on everyone, you know this. It's like a computer. So what do we need?' Mumble from the audience. 'I can't hear you? What do you need?'

'To upgrade!' chants the audience.

'That's right', says the very effective old-school motivational speaker on stage. 'And not just any upgrade. We need the right...'

'System!' chants the audience.

'Bingo!' he says. 'Get your core values, your core beliefs, your *operating system* updated, and then *everything* works better.'

I'm at a big public event called 'Upgrade to Success' (or something along those lines). I had scored myself a free ticket (supposedly valued at $997) to this two-day event, and by mid-morning I found myself marvelling at this success-merchant's methods. He had a fair few covert hypnosis methods in play, including sentence fragments that had the audience chanting in unison.

Sentence fragments (where you have to fill in some of the blanks of a spoken sentence) are designed to achieve a specific goal. By overloading your brain with questions about the missing parts of the sentence, the speaker is masterfully taking over your conscious thoughts with a wealth of subconscious queries.

In addition to this, the verbally embedded commands (or 'seeded suggestions') deliver one message to the conscious mind and another to the subconscious. This fools the average listener into believing the response was their own thought. And those were just a couple of the techniques he was using.

This style of hypnosis is powerful in the hands of such a pro. Even the most closed minds can be putty in the hands of someone like this.

So what's this all about? Ah, the reveal...

Some 40 minutes later, the success-merchant on stage begins plugging his 'Operation Success' program—essentially a DVD series and some books that will supposedly help you build the internal-belief operating system you need in order to achieve success. But lo! The shipment of this program didn't arrive in full. Gasp! This means there aren't enough programs available for everyone in the audience. Some of you will miss out if you don't act fast. Because the only way you can get the special, limited offer (with a bonus exclusive webinar and a special price of $997) is if you *buy today*...

I had previously spotted at least half a dozen 'plants' in the audience of a thousand or so, and at this point they get out of their seats and move swiftly to the back of the room to 'secure their purchase'.

Cue stampede.

It was perfectly orchestrated: this little act—the layering of commands, the anchoring of positive gesticulation towards the program, the reveal of scarcity and the exclusivity factor—is all too much. Before I know it, people are jostling past me, wide-eyed yet frantic-looking, desperate to secure their program.

In that one morning, this guy had probably sold half a million dollars' worth of programs.

Part of me loves that.

What a master! With no coercion, in only a few hours he had influenced the motivation and triggered his desired behaviour in a mass of people. Ingenious. I'd doff my hat to him, if I were wearing one.

Part of me loathes that.

What a manipulator! These programs aren't really worth $997 a pop. They're just part of a stepped program model, for which I'm sure the supposedly 'exclusive' webinar is just a sales tool — a piece that leads up to a 'billionaire boot camp' and a trusted 'inner circle' (one of the cornerstone techniques used by cult leaders).

But everything is manipulation.

Soon you'll see how everything, at some level, is motivational manipulation. Everything influences our behaviour, but most everything is just poorly designed (or barely designed at all). And when it's masterful, who are we to judge? The power is in the *intent*, and all we can do is operate with the best of it.

Success should never be the focus.

But intent aside, I still have issues with the word 'success' and the blind thinking the pursuit of it can create. And you should too. Particularly if you're leading teams. Why?

- **It's asymptotic.** Like mastery, success is something that's never really achieved. There's always more that can be done.

- **It blinds you.** Focusing on success — the achievement of a clear vision or a goal — can blind you to the opportunities and inherent joy of the journey.

- **Failures are devalued.** A focus on success can create a culture of intolerance to failure. A necessary part of any exploration, innovation and improvement is built on the cumulative learnings of mistakes and failures.

- **It's disempowering.** Lauding the successful, when done well, can trigger the inspiration that leads to aspiration. When done poorly, it can create a pedestal, where the successful look amazing; it's literally a maze for us to work out how they got there. We don't see the process and the effort that went into it—we see only the end result.

- **It won't make you happy.** Shawn Achor, a Harvard researcher and the author of *The Happiness Advantage*, argues that while success doesn't increase your chances of happiness, happiness does increase your chances of success.

This last point is key. You see, we've got it backwards—we need to find happiness in the *process*, not in the success. Happiness drives motivation, not success.

The secret to secrets (and other things you don't know)

Like sex, secrets sell. Just add the word 'secrets' to any article, blog or book title, along with a number, and you'll have a scientifically proven formula for increasing readership and open-rate.

Here, I'll show you:

Discover the 5 Little-Known Secrets Most Motivational Experts Don't Want You to Know!

Tempting, isn't it? Or maybe we can drop the formula and just go punchy:

Everything You Know About Motivation is WRONG.

Actually, Dan Pink uses this trick is his great book *Drive: The Surprising Truth About What Motivates Us.* More on this later (the book is brilliant, by the way).

The success-merchants and management consultants have been selling these secrets for centuries. And even I'm playing this card a bit. Why? Because it works.

There's a hidden truth to counterintuition. It works on savvy folk like you, who read books like this. Clive Thompson, a technology journalist and writer for *Wired* magazine, suggests that our willingness to have our basic beliefs overturned may actually be a sign of intellectual health. This lies at the heart of scientific enquiry: any challenge to your current knowledge paradigm will create a dissonance worth following up. 'Scientists understand that there's a good chance today's knowledge will eventually be proven wrong', Thompson argues. 'And good scientists welcome that prospect—they're thrilled by it.'

I hope you're thrilled too. But the concepts in this book are actually very pragmatic and grounded in reason.

There are no secrets, really, but there's a lot to motivation strategy and design that still remains *hidden*. Tucked away behind the noise and hype of what we have traditionally looked at, there is the essence of what really motivates us to progress through change and do great work.

To find this, we need to challenge our own conventional thinking and declare a war on 'just because'.

Declaring war on 'just because'

The real secret to unlocking better motivation to do the stuff that matters is to make doing the stuff that matters easier to do.

In chapter 3 we explore the concept of the big motivation gap—the thing between where you are and where you want to be. Most often this gap is full of friction.

Friction is the paperwork, the approval process, the waiting times, the pointless protocols, forgotten passwords, death by committees, bureaucratic nonsense and throbbing egos, and the ever-increasing information overload that we try to digest every day. Scott Belsky, author of *Making Ideas Happen,* believes this sort of friction is killing us 'with a thousand tiny paper cuts'.

Belsky further observes, 'Great creative leaders consider the contrarian view whenever something is being done "just because that's the way it's always been done".' The right interjection, or quest for clarification, made with conviction, could yield massive wins for your personal productivity and motivation.

It's like a spring clean.

Have you ever had the experience of returning home after a long holiday to think, 'I can't believe how messy the house is'? We don't notice the dust beginning to accumulate, along with the insidious entropy, until we get a new perspective.

Now, when was the last time you had a fresh look at the processes guiding behaviour at work?

The difference here is that most people spend most of their time working *in* the business. It's only on those rare occasions when you get a new executive hire, or participate in a conference or retreat, that you get a chance to look at what you are doing from a new perspective. At all other times, you're operating from *within* the game, and potentially blind to the opportunities that surround you.

Sometimes it pays to get someone in who is completely naive to your business and industry. Why? Because they will bring a fresh perspective.

If you bring in an expert with 20 years' experience in your industry, they may be blinded by the game they're playing. You need someone to ask those seemingly dumb but powerfully wise questions like 'Why is everyone working in a cubicle?' and 'Why aren't your action steps captured in your meetings, and why do they take so long?' and 'Why aren't these two guys collaborating and sharing that resource?' — and so on.

If you find yourself thinking, 'I don't know why we do it that way … it's just the way it is', then you've got yourself a new mission: find out why. Unearth the hidden truth.

If you discover there is no purpose to an activity, it's just a time-waster. You'll be able to change the game to get rid of it. But if you discover something's true purpose (perhaps a reason for longer meetings or for particular desk layouts), then you may be able to tweak elements of the game to improve it.

Like one of those old-school 'magic eye' books, sometimes the answers are staring us right in the face. We just need to shift our perspective a little, challenge our thinking, unearth the hidden gems and avoid the allure of quick fixes.

The allure of quick fixes

If something's not working, it makes sense to want to fix it. And quickly too. But the trouble with quick fixes to motivation is that they can often produce unintended consequences. Even when implemented with the best of intentions.

Imagine you're leading an organisational division through massive change. Your organisation sells enterprise software online, and you're halfway through transitioning from a deployment sales service (where your veteran business development experts would work up strategic sales solutions with big clients) to a 'software-as-a-service' model (where the customer downloads and trials the software for free, no salesperson required). The game is shifting from sales to support, and many in your team are getting their feathers ruffled. It means extra work for them, and more change, discomfort and uncertainty too. There's a tendency to resist these new changes, and even though the strategy has been debated rigorously, key staff still argue with the change.

And so we find ourselves grasping for quick fixes. Why?

- **To overcome the angst.** Change is hard, and sometimes the wrong quick fix is better than no fix. It feels like we're in control, and we're doing something. It eases the angst.

- **To maintain the equilibrium.** Game changing involves disruption, and people become uncomfortable with too much change. By resorting to an old faithful default-thinking quick fix, people can be fooled into thinking that the boat isn't rocking too much. After all, you still need work to be done during the period of change.

- **And besides, you're busy too.** Coming up with a fancy new motivation strategy can take time. And you won't always get it right in the first instance, either. So it will take time, when you specifically don't have time. And it won't be right anyway. So why put yourself through the pain? Why not stick with the tried-and-tested method? It's what most do.

But lo! We're changing the game here, and a good thing too.

This book aims to give you a new approach. And, while you and I would both prefer to be strategic and considered at all times, we both know that sometimes quick fixes are required.

It is my hope, though, that after your investment of time reading this, and getting the lowdown on what has been years of research and enquiry from me, you'll have the savvy to discover the game-changing element that'll improve things in the right way.

A QUICK NOTE ON SHINY IDEA SYNDROME

Similar to Shiny Object Syndrome (where one becomes addicted to the excitement of purchasing or obtaining new things), Shiny Idea Syndrome is a collection of symptoms that usually results in people getting overly excited by new ideas, at the expense of attention and focus on their *best* ideas.

It's what happens in conferences and meetings, where we are far removed from the friction and effort required to progress things in the real world. And it's great to be on the lookout for new ideas, but let's remember ...

New ideas can get in the way of your best ideas

Think about it: you've got a really clever idea you want to implement for your business, and you've made a great start. But then along comes a networking event or a conference, a new book or a conversation and then lo! you've got yourself another new and completely different idea. This new idea has allure and charm. It's enticing and sexy.

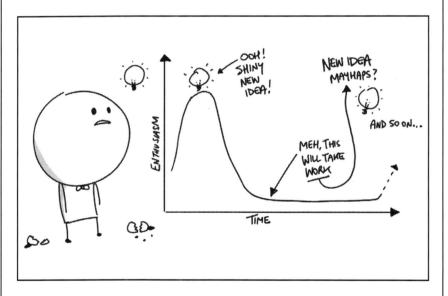

You start flirting with this new idea, and the honeymoon with your original idea begins to fade. Then, before you know it, you've worked yourself into a series of 'modern' relationships with new ideas, quickly moving from one idea to the next, spending time with them only while it's exciting, but never enough for there to be any meaningful progress.

This is a tricky situation to be in. As Thomas Edison once said, 'Genius is 1 per cent inspiration, 99 per cent perspiration'. New ideas actually help us avoid the 99 per cent bit, but perspiration (effort) is exactly what we need if we want to get our ideas where they need to go—reality.

The good news is that there's a way out. Here are some simple tips for maintaining healthy relationships with ideas:

1. **Be clear on your real objectives first.** Make ideas 'apply' for your attention by meeting your own criteria. What are your dating preferences for new ideas?

2. **Break ideas down into action steps.** *Idea* is often a glossy term for what can be a shirt-load of work. Turn your new idea into a real project plan, sleep on it, then see how sexy it really is first thing in the morning.

3. **Do more doing.** The fastest way to get to know your new ideas is to put them to work. It's survival of the fittest—any lame ideas will turn into learnings, and your best ideas may turn into real results.

4. **Share your actions, not your ideas.** Just talking about your ideas won't make them happen. Build accountability into the actions you need to take to make your ideas happen.

5. **Treat inspiring ideas with caution.** Ask yourself, does this idea really work for me, or is it just helping me avoid the 99 per cent bit? Get ruthlessly good at prioritising your ideas.

Motivation — strategy and design

Most of what you'll come across in motivation land is 'tactics'. 'Tips and tricks' can create short-term change, but it's your motivation strategy and design that'll make the difference.

Tactics are a bit like cooking ingredients

Each of them is great and benign in its own right. And when combined well they can make for some gloriously good cake. But combine the ingredients incorrectly, or cook them out of sequence, and things could go pear-shaped rather splendidly.

Strategy is having the savvy to identify the right ingredients and then mix them in the correct order.

What works in one context might not work in another. I'll show you what I mean.

In 2009, the very popular micro-blogging website Tumblr introduced an activity dashboard that displayed your overall popularity score, or 'tumblarity'. They hoped this game-changing element would help people to engage more with the platform, as increased engagement equalled a higher popularity. 'And engage they did', observes Sebastian Deterding (a genuine gamification expert), although the engagement was completely unintended.

'Since the easiest way to raise tumblarity was to just post as much as possible, the community previously characterised by careful curation of web curiosities got drowned in dribble—or so the community felt, and reacted with a huge backlash.' Less than one year later, Tumblr removed tumblarity altogether.

Does this mean points-based popularity tracking is bad? Heck no. It all depends on context. The auction site eBay uses a popularity score to rank sellers on factors such as promptness of delivery, accuracy of goods descriptions, and packaging. This works on eBay because the element is aligned to the motivations of both buyer and seller.

But with the introduction of any new element, there is an inherent risk of unintended consequences. The more quantitative and solid the element is, the more likely unintended consequences will manifest.

The Law of Unintended Consequences

Like Murphy's Law ('Anything that can go wrong, will go wrong', like how buttered toast always lands face down), the Law of Unintended Consequences describes the results from an action that could not be foreseen (otherwise the action might not have been taken). There are three main types of Unintended Consequence:

- **An unexpected positive outcome.** This is also known as serendipity or a windfall. For instance, the drug aspirin was created for pain relief, but it was also found to act as an anticoagulant and so was prescribed as a drug to help prevent heart attacks and thrombotic strokes.

- **A dastardly negative outcome.** The overall goal of the project has been achieved, but there is an additional unpleasant side effect that had not been anticipated. The cane toad did a mighty good job of combating the cane beetle when introduced into Australia, but now the cane toad runs the show in many ecosystems in northeastern Australia. They're like nasty little ugly gangsters.

- **A perverse or contrary outcome.** The overall aim has not been achieved, and in fact a side effect has compounded or exacerbated the original problem. This is most commonly known nowadays as the Streisand Effect, after the American entertainer tried to suppress photos of her Malibu pad, but instead only generated further publicity and attention.

We can apply the same logic to motivation. I like to think of it as a 'shadow side': for every positive action you take to influence motivation, there's a shadow effect that we need to be aware of.

For example, if you drop in a reward bonus to motivate staff, you might get an increase in focus and drive (achieving the aim of the tool), but potentially this will be at the cost of creativity and collaboration. Add an annual recognition program for high achievers, and you'll get an increase in performance (potentially for some), but that might be at the cost of disengagement, resentment and politics within the organisation.

This stuff is largely unavoidable, but it can be managed through the right motivation strategy and design. And good strategy and design comes from ...

Relentless iteration

Just as flying a group of executives to an exotic island to cook up the 'perfect' strategy won't create change automatically, neither will simply reading a book or attending a course or conference.

You need to start to put insights into action, and work up your own game plan to iterate and improve ruthlessly. *Good design is 80 per cent iteration.*

The irony of expertise, and this book

Just as the plumber's taps are always leaking, the mechanic's car breaks down and the emotional intelligence expert is in therapy for anger management, this motivation design expert went through all sorts of crap to produce this book.

Pretty much every form of self-sabotage imaginable was road-tested in the preparation of this book. I've included some insights for you in chapter 7.

Ignorance is bliss

It's terribly ironic, but fairly inescapable. And guess what – you're about to feel it too. Ignorance, when it comes to motivation design, is bliss. Read on and you'll never be able to view motivation or behaviour in the same way again. You'll never be able to experience the naive joy delivered by inspirational speakers, or the keen excitement of discovering new motivation 'secrets'. You'll also never be able to claim that the solution is simply down to values and attitudes, or beyond your ability to solve or influence.

Instead, every motivation, behaviour or cultural challenge is soon to become a puzzle to you. A frustrating riddle to be solved, with the answer sometimes lying hidden in plain sight.

But, if the magazines in planes are anything to go by, the world loves a good puzzle. The sudoku and crosswords are always attacked with vigour. Why shouldn't motivation be the same?

YOU HAVE THE ANSWERS — NOW RUB THAT DUCK

Here's a useful activity you can try the next time you're stuck on what to do. You may be trying to progress through your own project, shift the motivational dynamics of a team or deal with particular behaviours you've observed at work.

In any event, 'rubber-ducking' is a great technique to have up your sleeve, and it isn't half as rude as it sounds! We might even call it a game, since it involves two players, one active (you) and the other not so much.

This technique originated from a coder who kept a rubber duck near his monitor. Every time he came across a really complex coding problem, he'd explain it to his duck. Through the long, uninterrupted explanation, he'd often stumble across (or trigger) a thought that opened up a pathway to a solution.

The technique is incredibly useful if you're dealing with a level of complexity that's too hard to explain to someone who's not in the thick of it. You know what I mean. You spend so much time trying to get them to *understand* the problem, and warding off well-intended but overly simple and flawed advice you've already dismissed, that you throw up your hands in surrender, more frustrated than when you started.

Rubber-ducking solves that, but it needs some framing.

First, find an introverted friend or a colleague who can keep quiet. This can be very hard to do. Then find a cafe or destination (ideally with cupcakes) that's 20 to 40 minutes' walk away. Frame things up with your colleague or friend: 'I've got this challenge. I don't know what the answer is just yet. But I'd like to just walk it through with you. Your reward will be a cupcake and coffee at this fancy cafe a good walk away. But on the way there I'm going to talk to you. At you. About this challenge I've got. I don't want you to say anything. Just nod and listen. Maybe make some "hrmm" sounds. I'll work it out by the time we get there, and then we can have a good chat on the way back.'

Give it a go. You'll be surprised at how the contextual shift can unearth a lot of solutions you already had. If you've got a particularly helpful friend, the walk back can focus on how you're going to make your solution happen — the steps required to make it happen.

Just don't do this all the time. I've learned that occasionally you need to show interest in other people's lives in order to maintain friendships. True fact.

Don't take things too seriously

'Seriousness' is a form of defence that protects us from exposure to risk. It's easy to be bland, just another suit in a sea of suits, criticising new ideas from the safety of the sidelines.

But if you're on the field — if you're changing the game — there's nowhere to hide. Your performance is monitored, and you are accountable for your actions. You stand out. Your mistakes will be noticed. It's scary, but it's the only place to play if you want to be making progress.

To stay progressive, you need to stay playful. Einstein once said that play is the highest form of research. It's experimentation and learning in its purest form. Curiosity is the companion to meaningful change.

 CHAPTER SUMMARY

So, in this chapter we've forayed through the fog of folklore that surrounds motivation — individually and at work. Some classic clichés were busted, and you can now see through the veil. You're in the right place to start finding the game changer that will influence motivation, shift behaviour and shape culture. Scientifically so.

We've seen how science gets warped into folklore and have exposed the dangers of positive thinking and self-belief. We've unpacked a way for you to move forward without conviction or belief, and we've ditched 'success' as our focus. You've been given a couple of ways to think differently about motivation and behaviour challenges — but we're just getting started.

AN IMPERATIVE FOR CHANGE

No matter how amazing an idea is until proven otherwise, its imagined benefits will pale in comparison to the real, and unimagined, fear of change… This creates an unfortunate paradox: the greater the potential of an idea, the harder it is to find anyone willing to try it.

— Scott Berkun

Now that we have waded through the swamp of motivational folklore, let's put the focus back on what we want to actually get people motivated about — meaningful progress and change.

Change, huh.

Now there's a tricky concept. I'm tempted to get all existential here, but let's keep it real: whether we like it or not, stuff is changing all around us, all the time. And unless you've been hiding in a cave, you'll know that industries, technology, distractions, demographics — just about everything — is constantly changing. And the rate of change is getting faster (which, ironically, is one thing that hasn't changed over time).

I grew up in the golden years before 'teh Internets' was invented, and 'lol kittehs' existed only in real life. I remember playing music on tape cassettes. I used to make good mix-tapes, sitting by the radio waiting for the right song to come along, then hitting the play and record buttons at the same time so I could capture it on the cassette. I thought my Walkman was so cool, but then the Discman came out — a portable compact-disc player! Incredible. I remember taking a jog with the Discman once — the CD would hold about an hour's worth of music, but you needed to keep it flat, otherwise the disc would skip (making you look like a running butler holding a serving tray).

It was not so effective as a running assistant — and besides, now my iPhone holds several months' worth of music. And my running is now geo-tracked. And I get to play a game called *Zombies, Run!* (which makes you feel like you're literally being chased by the zombies).

When I was younger, none of this would have seemed possible. Soon we'll switch from wearable tech like Google Glass (optics with an in-built, internet-linked phone and display) to embedded technology and augmented reality. And things'll keep changing fast. Whatever field you are in, a handful of new disruptive start-ups will have appeared overnight while you slept. Sure, most of these will fail, but some may threaten (or enhance) the business you're in.

It's all about staying ahead of the game.

In nature, the most resilient and successful species are the ones with the ability to respond and adapt to change. You snooze, you lose.

But I daresay you know that. There are plenty of books out there that talk about the need to change. We all get it. And, if you were to talk to most people, few would argue that improving an existing process or situation, or exploring and capitalising on opportunities, is a bad thing. The issue of contention, when it comes to change, is how it's managed and achieved.

Everybody loves change, right?

We love change, so long as it's not happening to us. While we can all agree on the *premise* of change, and that change drives innovation and growth, where we get tripped up is in its *execution*.

Change is usually accompanied by a heap of uncertainty. We don't like uncertainty, and in the absence of any good structure we will cling to what we know. This, in most cases, happens to be the status quo.

Broadly speaking, organisations tend to go one of two ways when managing change.

On one side, organisations moving through change plough ahead, leaving people to fend for themselves without any structure or clarity. Goals, roles and responsibilities shift, and people are left guessing what will happen next. Staff learn to be conservative with the effort they invest in their work, as they are uncertain if:

a   their work will make a meaningful and relevant contribution if goals and targets are just going to shift anyway

b   they have the authority to make decisions as roles change

c   they even have a future in the company (is it even worth investing effort in longer-term projects?).

The alternative approach some organisations take is to clog up systems and processes with endless new meetings and procedures. Here, employee time and initiative is eroded, and the pace of change becomes glacial. Things get ever more bureaucratic and political, and people learn to resent the change. 'Why can't we just go back to the old way of doing things?' they ask.

John Kotter, a Harvard Business School Professor of Leadership, argues that most major change and transformation initiatives generate only lukewarm results (or fail miserably). Why? Kotter suggests that too many managers and leaders forget that transformation is a process, not an isolated event. It takes time.

Change is hard

In a 2006 *Harvard Business Review* essay, 'Leading Change', Kotter identifies the main ways transformation and change get derailed within organisations. And he's spot-on. The essay is still very relevant today. Many of these barriers apply to smaller teams, and some can apply to individual efforts as well. I have anchored most of this section to Kotter's key points, adding in some more contemporary examples, and insight from a motivation strategy and design perspective.

If it's not urgent, it's not important

Management consultant and author Stephen Covey is famous for popularising the distinction between the things that are important and the things that are urgent. 'Most of us spend too much time on what is urgent and not enough time on what is important', he says. And it's true — the urgent always outweighs the important in terms of the demands it makes on our attention. Just watch what most people do when they're working away on an important task and their phone rings on the other side of the room. Many of us will abandon the task and crash through the furniture to answer it in time (even though it's likely to be unimportant).

But often the difference between urgency and importance is simply *structure*.

Urgent things have a deadline and a sense of priority. They are often attached to some form of accountability. They have mechanisms that trigger you to act, and a raft of structural motivation elements that many of the important activities lack.

This can create a vicious cycle, with the urgent constantly getting in the way of the important. In chapter 3 we'll unpack the process of short-circuiting this; moving from automation (the status quo of a functioning system) to aspiration (the precursor to motivation and change).

Change is not a single-player game

If you're wanting to don the cape and turn around an organisation singlehandedly... you're possibly deluded in a not-so-useful way. The best adventurers have companions, and leading change in a large enterprise is going to take more than a single individual. You don't have all of the answers, nor do you have all of the clout and influence needed to progress transformational change.

Kotter calls this group of change agents the 'guiding coalition'. And, because it is likely that this group will (indeed, it should) include members who are not part of senior management, the group will tend to operate outside of the normal organisational hierarchy. 'This can be awkward,' Kotter argues, 'but it is clearly necessary. If the existing hierarchy were working well, there would be no need for a major transformation. But since the current system is not working, reform generally demands activity outside of formal boundaries, expectations, and protocol'.

So how do you get this guiding coalition together? Someone needs to create a sense of urgency around the concept of change — keeping it out of the too-hard basket and off the 'we'll deal with it later' shelf. And because change requires strategy, which requires immersion, these things cannot be achieved within the confines of normal, everyday work.

You'll need to create 'rally points', moments in time when the right people gather outside of the context of normal work. 'Off-site retreats, for two or three days, are one popular vehicle for accomplishing this task', Kotter observes. 'I have seen many groups of five to 35 executives attend a series of these retreats over a period of months.'

I have facilitated more than a few executive retreats in my time — from senior executives of technology companies going through massive change, to the directors of multiple medical organisations moving to amalgamate their businesses into one entity (with all of the cultural integration challenges that brings). There are a few things that are key to getting this right:

1. Shift the context and disrupt the pattern

The space needs to be conducive to lateral discussion. Therefore, meeting in the company's boardroom or in the same conference venue that annual meetings are held just won't cut it. We want to disrupt existing patterns of thought, to literally put people into a place of comfortable discomfort.

In some of the retreats I've been involved in, executives would meet on exotic islands — to spend the whole time cooped up indoors in another 'me too' conference venue. With the same curtains, carpets, free mints and bad coffee that are common to most conference venues. In situations like this, we need to disrupt the existing pattern, and get participants involved in activities that facilitate breakthrough thinking.

2. Keep it diverse

Before running any retreats, the guiding coalition must be formed. This is best developed organically, through discussion and over time. The group will gain momentum, but before you start making big strategic decisions you'll want to ensure you're getting a good diversity of input.

I was once involved with strategy facilitation of the senior executive team from a multinational organisation that needed to transition their whole sales approach, address the gap of non-existent succession planning, get more regional diversity in their emerging leadership, and develop talent attraction and recruitment strategies. The thing is, the whole executive team comprised Caucasian males over 50 years old. You can do better than a team that consists entirely of stale pale males!

3. Keep it clean

Inevitably, agendas are going to become contaminated by personal agendas. Yours too. It's largely unavoidable. A strong personality in a position of influence can start to play political games and skew things in a self-serving direction. Very likely it'll still be good development—but it won't be as good as if all perspectives are considered.

This is where an experienced, expert facilitator comes in. If you're organising a series of retreats, a good facilitator will provide structure and help guide the process in a way that is most conducive to genuine progress.

I say *expert* facilitator quite deliberately—you want a facilitator who has the right expertise (not one who simply keeps meetings running smoothly and to the agenda). This facilitator will need to be able to set the appropriate framing of the day, establishing clear contexts to keep people focused on the stuff that matters. They'll need to know when to move the agenda forward and when to hold the tension, warding off our desire to default to quick fixes, and instead going deep to unearth the real issues and opportunities.

4. Go deep

Strategic retreats have a massive opportunity cost attached to them. Taking key people — usually the high performers and difference makers — out of their organisational roles for a day or three will mean their productivity takes a huge hit. So the imperative is to make sure these retreats are effective.

But the danger here is that the inherent difficulty of making change work can see us become superficial, jumping to another set of quick fixes, rather than staying with the uncertainty and getting to the root cause of the problem (and the best pathway to change).

A good retreat will have a loose agenda and a flexible expert facilitator, able to work with the group to get the best thinking and outcomes (not simply the easiest or quickest ones). This usually involves the use of different 'games' — temporal structures and constraints designed to bring about better thinking. This sometimes involves asking questions like, 'If we were to start this business again today from scratch, what would we do differently?' or 'What would Google do? Or Batman? Or da Vinci?'

5. Accelerate trust

Trust is developed over a series of interactions. It's slow to build, and easy to break. And it's not so much a case of making one big 'trust-building' gesture or declaration — they often seem contrived. It's more a case of accumulating trust through many micro-interactions between people. And this means getting people together in the same room, and using the gaps within the agenda to full advantage. It's the breakfasts, dinners, drinks and 'non-formal' periods of interaction that often serve to accelerate trust most effectively.

6. Scaffold the journey

As things change faster, it's getting increasingly hard to predict what the next disruption will be.

Most strategy is done deliberately. 'Failing to plan is planning to fail', the old adage goes. And so the temptation is to head off to a retreat with senior leaders and cook up the perfect plan with which to ambush the rest of the organisation.

This book favours a much more agile/emergent approach to strategy and change. An evolving collection of strategic experiments gives leaders more choices, which—compared to investing all efforts in the creation of one 'perfect plan'—means better odds that some of the choices will be right.

Management theorist Henry Mintzberg makes a distinction between old-school 'deliberate' planning and the relatively contemporary emergent approach to strategy. *Deliberate strategy* relies on senior leaders to set goals and develop plans and strategies to achieve them. Deliberate strategy is goal-oriented. It asks, 'What do we want to achieve?'

Emergent strategy, on the other hand, is means-oriented and asks, 'What is possible with the means we have at our disposal?' Here we have a strategy that emerges from all over the company, over time, as the environment changes and the organisation shifts and adapts to apply its strengths to a changing reality. Emergent strategy is an organic approach to growth that lets companies learn and continually develop new strategies over time based on an ongoing culture of hypothesis and experimentation.

At some point strategic retreats need to translate into action. And the best way for this action to take shape, and inform emerging strategy, is if it is conducted as a series of *experiments*.

A vision needs to be captured

The *promise* provided by change needs to be stronger than the *premise* under which you're currently operating. The aspiration needs to be greater than the resistance. A vision helps to inspire and capture aspiration, and assist people in overcoming the inherent inertia associated with moving away from the known and familiar. Also, a clear vision helps to ensure alignment with projects and experiments conducted—it's easier to know if a project is in line with a vision if your vision is clearly defined.

But here's the thing: a clearly defined vision does not have to mean a *specific* one. In fact, I'd strongly recommend against making your strategic visions too bold and specific, as it will only serve to narrow your thinking, hobbling your agility.

Rather, you want to keep your vision clear and easy to identify with.

Microsoft's vision used to be very clear and compelling: 'A computer on every desk and in every home, running Microsoft software.' Today, not so much. Before retiring, Microsoft CEO Steve Ballmer announced the new vision: 'Going forward, our strategy will focus on creating a family of devices and services for individuals and businesses that empower people around the globe at home, at work and on the go, for the activities they value most.' Technology strategist Ben Thompson observes that Microsoft's new vision is 'so bland as to be meaningless'. He further asks, 'What is going to motivate employees working on a huge array of products whose contributions are so far removed from the all-up Profit & Loss?'

For Thompson, Apple, the essential counterexample, tends to anchor its vision on things more, well, visionary. Take Apple's advertising slogan from 1997, 'Think Different' (which you can easily watch on YouTube):

> Here's to the crazy ones. The misfits. The rebels. The troublemakers. The round pegs in the square holes...

Thompson observes: 'The truth about the greatest commercial of all time—Think Different—is that the intended audience was Apple itself. Steve Jobs took over a demoralised company on the precipice of bankruptcy. This vision reminded them that they were special, and that Jobs was special. It was the beginning of a new chapter: Think Different.'

Around this time, Steve Jobs had introduced a very different style of thinking to Apple's extensive product line. Jobs drew a classic four-quadrant chart, *consumer* and *pro* on one axis, *desktop* and *laptop* on the other, and then said, 'We are going to make one computer for each quadrant and we are going to kill all of the other product lines'. Bam. Thinking differently, with congruence between the vision and the strategy.

But back to a motivation perspective, Apple is uniquely reliant on non-monetary motivation; its employees genuinely believe they are making products that impact people's lives. The most recent campaign under CEO Tim Cook is likewise primarily designed for Apple employees. Now, the focus is on excellence and the quality of Apple's design.

In some of the vision-crafting sessions I've run with executives, there has been a tendency to collapse things into lame corporate speak. Things have numbers attached to them. Meaningless, distant numbers. It's safe, serious, bland and uninspiring. It's the type of thing that would end up framed in reception — 'Our Vision is to collaboratively maintain long-term high-impact supply chains beyond compliance while fostering organic innovation strategies that engage staff, clients and stakeholders to participate in uniquely positioned multifaceted niche market systems'. Bleh! Or it'd be dryly shared with the troops during a conference. Either way, a thing to be largely ignored.

Unearthing the real vision takes work. But it's work worth doing because both the vision and the narrative attached to it will become the contextual rally point throughout the process of change. It's the social artefact that's shared across the organisation. It's the *purpose piece* that gets referred to when things are going astray.

But of course, coming up with a magic vision among the team on a retreat is one thing; communicating it to the wider organisation as the narrative and imperative for change is quite another.

The rationale for change needs to be communicated

Sending out a big email after cooking up a mean vision won't see change happen. 'We've put the vision on the intranet', one client told me. Others will say they've printed it out and put it in the staff room. Wow.

But Ballmer (then CEO of Microsoft) takes the cake once again. In 2013 Ballmer wrote an email of over 2700 words (note: an *email*), describing his new vision and strategy for a 'far-reaching realignment of the company that will enable us to innovate with greater speed, efficiency and capability in a fast changing world'. It was quite an informative email — but still, to many it was a big ambush bomb full of proposed changes, finishing up on a stirring note (there — now go be inspired). The intention may have been good, but the execution was poor, and mainly served to amuse The Internets.

Kotter shares similar experiences. 'I've seen three patterns with respect to communication, all very common. In the first, a group actually does develop a pretty good transformation vision and then proceeds to communicate it by holding a single meeting or sending out a single communication. Having used about 0.0001% of the yearly intracompany communication budget, the group is startled when few people seem to understand the new approach.'

To make change really work, you will need to use every possible channel available to you to communicate the vision. Unfortunately, within most organisations, conventional communications are so junked up with standard, non-essential communications that it'd be difficult to really get any cut through. Or people have learned to ignore them.

One client I've worked with (alongside behavioural scientists, psychologists and designers from Pragmatic Thinking, a behaviour and motivation strategy company) had a tricky situation: trust in management was traditionally low, as was faith in the standard communications channels. In order to get cut through for a major internal motivation and behaviour strategy program we were implementing, we needed to do some guerilla marketing. This included coasters, posters, comics and other novel material in addition to conventional communications. We created a 'brand within a brand' and used humour to communicate what was really on everyone's minds.

In chapter 4 we unpack why we humans are naturally conservative with the effort we invest in things. If communication doesn't happen (through multiple channels, at multiple times and in high volume), it is unlikely people will want to invest effort in the process of change (even if they are unhappy with the status quo).

Vision? Check. Communication? Check. Now what?

Well, that's the easy stuff over. Now we need to actually empower people to act on the vision.

And how do we do that?

Well, we need to get people taking action and driving projects in alignment with the vision. This sometimes means making it safe for people to take risks and engage in non-standard activities and experiments. Much of this book is dedicated to understanding how to progress change like this through conducting evolving experiments (and managing motivation throughout).

Occasionally, you'll encounter powerful individuals who vehemently resist change. There are many ways to tackle this: remove them, persuade them, distract them, involve them, and so on. You can invest a lot of effort in the politics of change; but if you focus on getting the process of change right, the rest usually falls into place.

Once people are empowered to act upon the vision—to begin to play a new game—we need to amplify and reinforce the new behaviours we want to see. This involves celebrating small wins early, making progress visible (more on this in chapter 4).

From there, we consolidate any improvements to produce more momentum and change, using evidence collected from earlier experiments to support continued effort (and investment) in progress and change. And then, with the momentum of evidence collected, new behaviours become normalised. The New Way of Doing Things is clearly articulated and linked to corporate success.

Easy, right? In theory, yes. But there's a *paradox* for leaders that makes it hard in practice.

A paradox for leaders

What's the difference between a leader and a manager?

In his 1989 book *On Becoming a Leader*, Warren Bennis composed a list of the key differences between a leader and a manager, along the following lines. These distinctions are still used today.

> The manager administers; the leader innovates.
> The manager is a copy; the leader is an original.
> The manager maintains; the leader develops.
> The manager focuses on systems and structure; the leader focuses on people.
> The manager relies on control; the leader inspires trust.
> The manager has a short-range view; the leader has a long-range perspective.
> The manager asks how and when; the leader asks what and why.
> The manager imitates; the leader originates.
> The manager accepts the status quo; the leader challenges it.
> The manager does things right; the leader does the right thing.

The thing is, I don't think any of these distinctions between leaders and managers are really that helpful. Viewed through a modern filter, they're now quite rubbish concepts — because you can't really have one without the other.

When leaders forget how to manage and do things well, nothing happens. And when managers forget how to lead and inspire, nothing changes or improves. To successfully lead and manage an organisation through change, we need to bring together the best of both leadership and management.

The distinction between leaders and managers is a byproduct of the industrial revolution. Scott Berkun, author of *The Myths of Innovation* and other great books, suggests that despite how progressive some modern management programs are, their roots are in a tradition most unkind to innovation. 'Management as a discipline is steeped in an old-school command and control attitude that is alive and well in the Internet Age', Berkun argues.

It's time to abolish those roots, and the dualism of leaders and managers.

In our new and future economy, where value comes increasingly from the knowledge of people, workers are no longer simply cogs in an industrial machine. Management and leadership are no longer easily separated. People now look to their managers not simply to do prescribed tasks, but to define a purpose for them. Managers, in turn, must manage their people not just to maximise efficiency, but to nurture and grow talent and inspire results.

The late management expert Peter Drucker suggested that we don't 'manage' people any more. 'The task is to lead people', he wrote. 'And the goal is to make productive the specific strengths and knowledge of every individual.'

The Valve example

In 2012 the employee handbook from the popular video game and entertainment software developer Valve was 'leaked' to the internet. This well-designed book shared insights into the inner workings of an organisation with no hierarchy (it's flat) and very few rules.

Here's a snippet from one of the opening chapters of the book, welcoming new employees to 'Flatland':

> Hierarchy is great for maintaining predictability and repeatability. It simplifies planning and makes it easier to control a large group of people from the top down, which is why military organisations rely on it so heavily.

> But when you're an entertainment company that's spent the last decade going out of its way to recruit the most intelligent, innovative, talented people on Earth, telling them to sit at a desk and do what they're told obliterates 99 percent of their value. We want innovators, and that means maintaining an environment where they'll flourish.

A flat structure removes the organisational barriers that prevent good collaborative work from occurring. Valve models a blend of collaboratively driven self-leadership and self-management that we rarely see at work. And yet it has been recognised as so effective that the management structure has now become a reference point in modern MBA courses.

The handbook covers specific challenges prompted by the lack of a traditional structure, particularly around how to determine what projects to work on, and how to execute personal initiative. These include:

Balancing short-term and long-term goals

Without any overt hierarchy and structure, an organisation or team is able to respond rapidly to any opportunities to achieve business goals, or to stave off any potential threats that will clearly cost the business. This is great, but it carries the risk that everyone will be running around chasing the little things, putting out small fires very responsively, and not thinking proactively about longer-term goals. 'So our lack of a traditional structure comes with an important responsibility. It's up to all of us to spend effort focusing on what we think the long-term goals of the company should be', the handbook states.

Dealing with perceived hierarchy in a flat structure

The Valve Employee Handbook also discusses situations in which you may be told to work (or stop working) on something. And the person who has told you has been around for a long time. What do you do? Valve's answer is quite simple:

> The correct response to this is to keep thinking about whether or not your colleagues are right. Broaden the conversation. Hold on to your goals if you're convinced they're correct. Check your assumptions. Pull more people in. Listen. Don't believe that anyone holds authority over the decision you're trying to make. They don't; but they probably have valuable experience to draw from, or information/data that you don't have, or insight that's new. When considering the outcome, don't believe that anyone but you is the 'stakeholder'. You're it. And Valve's customers are who you're serving. Do what's right for them.

They keep their purpose in mind at all times, and don't let perceived hierarchical barriers get in the way of progress-making work.

Productivity without management?

One might wonder how anything gets done in a workplace where no one is telling anyone what they need to do or monitoring their performance. And one might wonder how they can manage all of the things that aren't getting done (because without structure, tasks will breed). Valve is quite empathetic to this:

> It's natural in this kind of environment to constantly feel like you're failing because for every one task you decide to work on, there will be dozens that aren't getting your attention. Trust us, this is normal. Nobody expects you to devote time to every opportunity that comes your way. Instead, we want you to learn how to choose the most important work to do.

The handbook goes on to detail how performance reviews and remuneration are handled, how to manage working from home, and what to do if you screw up (and you will—there is a high tolerance for failure). It even goes into detail about how the desks have wheels, so that you can organically create and dismantle collaborative work hubs. Literally every rule, structure or process 'friction' between Valve's staff and the organisation's objective (making great products for their customers) has been removed to better meet the vision.

The world is becoming flat

It would be easy to dismiss something like the Valve Employee Handbook as 'just another techie thing', like Google's now famous 20 per cent time, or other software developers' innovation hack days. 'It's easy for them — they're young and innovative, not like our [industry/company/organisation].'

But no matter which way you look at it, the world — and organisational hierarchy as we know it — is becoming flatter. As we mature beyond the industrial revolution into the new economy, the lines between leadership and management are becoming blurred. It's now about robots versus ninjas.

It's robots vs ninjas

Work is changing. In the main, whether in a factory, as an office clerk or in many other jobs, work used to consist of simple, routine, mundane and repetitive tasks. And because there was seemingly little that was inherently motivating about the work, it was reasoned that the only way to get people to do stuff was to incentivise them properly and monitor them closely.

But work has changed dramatically and is still changing. It's getting more complex — and the structures that worked to motivate people through routine work just don't work so well for the creative, collaborative and non-formulaic work of the future.

We've looked at the motivational folklore, and at the paradox of management and leadership through change. We'll cover motivation in a bit more detail in the next chapter, but here let's have a quick look at how the nature of work is changing.

Work can be divided into two main categories: 'algorithmic' and 'heuristic'. Algorithmic work involves routine tasks with predictable outcomes. Just as with some algebra puzzles, if you know what the answer is, you can work out what the steps are to balance the equation. On the flip side, you know exactly what type of outputs you'll get with what you put in. You can follow an established set of instructions through to its logical conclusion. Just like a robot.

But here's the thing: if you're doing robot work, your job may be at risk from real robots, machines and software.

In the manufacturing world this has been a trend for manual workers for several decades. Automotive factories, for example, were transformed by industrial robotics during the 1980s and they now routinely use machines to do specialist tasks that were once performed by humans, such as welding and spray painting. With driverless cars being perfected as you read this, the robotic possibilities are seemingly endless.

Robot work is getting automated and outsourced

Way back, I used to enter receipts for my business manually. My parents had taught me that it was important, and that all the little things, like all that coffee I enjoy, can be claimed to offset the tax implications associated with company's profit. But... I'm not too motivated to look after details like that. Indeed, I could hack my own motivation to do that, but... meh. It's little bits of paper with numbers on it. I've got better things to do with my time.

So I hired a low-level (journeyman) bookkeeper. They did a marvellous job, and quite frankly I don't know how I ran my company in the early days without one. But damn, it meant that I had to pay money for someone to enter these things for my accountant. There's got to be a more efficient way to do things, right?

And there is. We now simply collect all receipts across all activities, put them into an envelope and send them off to a company that scans it in with a computer. It's uncannily accurate in most instances, and incredibly efficient compared to paying someone to enter all of the details manually. It just makes sense.

A lot of robot-work like this is getting systematised and automated. Heck, even your inbox can be checked and attended to by intelligent, trainable algorithms (where a piece of software decides what to delete, archive or reply to with a simple message). Why go through the pain of employing ten or 20 people to manually process payroll, when one person operating a piece of software can do the job much more efficiently?

And here's the other thing: that one person doesn't need to be working in the same building as you. The intellectual labour required to manage these tasks is increasingly being outsourced to highly intelligent and capable people living in countries with a substantially lower cost of living.

The large consulting firm McKinsey & Co estimates that only 30 per cent of all job growth in the US now comes from robot (algorithmic) work; the rest comes from heuristic work. This figure is comparable to those of many developed countries with a high cost of living. The reason? Motivation expert Daniel Pink says, 'Routine work can be outsourced or automated; artistic, empathic, non-routine work generally cannot'.

And this puts us into the domain of ninja work — the stuff that can't be done by robots, or by the rule-abiding samurai within organisations.

Samurai

Whereas robots can work as unthinking non-innovators who persist with an inherited work dogma (at risk of being replaced by a cheaper robot, or a literal one), samurai are a bit different. In the context of this book, a samurai is a human who acts like a robot, but in an honourable way.

You will undoubtedly know people like this. They will go to great lengths to achieve their goal, but are ultimately honour-bound to follow orders. Samurai cannot break the rules or traditions, and they have an extreme intolerance of failure. So much so that samurai who fail are obliged to commit *hara kiri*, an honourable suicide by their own sword.

Noble as it may seem, this inflexibility is anathema to any rogue or ninja, and the heuristic work they do.

Ah, there's that word again: *heuristic*. It's the opposite of the algorithmic work that defined much of the industrial revolution, in that there is no formula. You need to experiment to discover the path that will best achieve the objective. It is otherwise undefined, and you have to come up with something new.

Rogues

I have a thing for ninjas and rogues. You can probably tell. Whenever I'm engaged in a roleplaying game, they're the archetypical character class I'll always choose. Wizards, oh they have their systems that make things work like magic. Warriors, they have their strength, directness and persistence. And priests, well... they have their faith (and the ability to detect lies and banish the undead, always handy). But rogues, ah, they are the clever ones. The ones who think laterally and take the path of least resistance to achieve their objectives.

THE BENEFITS OF EMPLOYING THE SERVICES OF A ROGUE

If you've got a great aspiration, goal or idea, you'll inevitably meet some obstacles while attempting to make it happen. Most of the time, you'll find your own way to navigate through the problems you encounter. But sometimes things can become so utterly stuck within existing processes that they go nowhere.

Your unfinished projects make a mockery of the time and resources you've already invested in them. It's not your fault—you're doing all the right things. But no matter how many meetings you have, nothing happens.

Now, you could hire a management consultant from an established firm, who also has an MBA and six decades of experience. But there's a good chance you'll receive recommendations that you will have already considered. After all, it's your business. You know the right ways to make things happen.

But sometimes the 'right' ways to fix problems just don't work. Sometimes it pays to hire, recruit or think like a rogue to help liberate and progress your ideas.

Here's why...

1. They think differently

Rogues operate outside of the conventional and established norms. They bend the rules, take shortcuts and generally screw with the system. Which is a good thing, because your organisational systems and established ways of doing things are often the very source of your problems. Systems resist ideas.

It's as Einstein once quipped: 'We cannot solve our problems with the same thinking we used when we created them.' He'd know—he was one of the greatest academic rogues of all time. If he had been working as a physicist instead of a clerk, he'd never have turned academia upside down.

2. They're not *heroes*

The last thing you want is a hero-consultant from a big firm coming in and 'putting things right'. Heroes blunder in to save the day. If there's nothing they can save, they'll make something up. And this means that they can zealously 'fix' things within your business before they even know if it needs fixing. When the dust settles, you'll be left wondering what happened, and whose victory it is.

Rogues play a supporting role. They always case the joint first, spending time working out what the real issue is. They find pathways, disarm traps, charm guards and point the way to help make your ideas happen. They can be heroic while letting you remain the hero.

3. They find the path of least resistance

This is perhaps where rogues got their bad name. In an era when patience and hard work were virtuous, those who took shortcuts or strayed from convention were frowned upon.

But in today's fast-paced economy, it's innovate or die. Sometimes, there isn't time to do things the right way. Sometimes we need to find the best way, and the secret shortcut may lie hidden right beneath you. It takes a fresh, external perspective to help you discover it.

4. They're objective-focused

When you're trying to make an idea happen, it's easy for you or your team to get distracted. Ideas get old very quickly, and the charm and allure of new ideas can distract anyone from the path of implementation.

Rogues, however, keep an eye on their mark. Remember, the system resists new ideas. Everyone's busy, and there are always fires that need putting out. But, if you're looking to execute ideas and achieve objectives faster, a rogue can see through this and keep you on track.

5. They're (somewhat) immune to politics

Sometimes it's that nasty subculture within your organisation that chokes the life out of any new ideas. Sometimes the things that block your ideas from happening are some of the very people you work with. You know what I'm talking about, but you don't want to point the finger.

(continued)

As an external and objective operative, a rogue brings a level of diplomatic immunity to the job. They can highlight issues that would otherwise be denounced in a cross-functional or ego feud. And once these issues are out in the open, they can rapidly move things into a more productive space.

6. They work to strengths

You won't see a rogue trying to do everything, though that's what some leaders attempt to do. They work to people's strengths. They unite diverse 'specialists' to get things done. Think *Ocean's 11* or *Mission Impossible*: you've got the espionage girl, the lock-pick guy, the explosives specialist, the techie, the planted agent, and so on.

There's no reason your team can't work like that too.

7. They question authority

This is probably why people are uncomfortable hiring rogues — they'll ask you questions. If you're hiring a non-conventional consultant external to your industry or business, chances are they'll ask you questions that seem dumb or obvious.

If they're a savvy operator, what they'll be doing is testing your assumptions, finding those gaps and inconsistencies within your own belief systems on how things should be done. Many of us don't realise that, as human beings, we are profoundly adept at getting in our own way. Taking on a rogue means you'll rethink your perspective on things (which is always a good thing).

Now, you're probably wondering — who are these rogues? In the gaming world, a rogue is someone who scouts ahead, disarms traps, picks locks and removes obstacles so that the main party can achieve their objectives. In the real world, you can think of a rogue as an external consultant or an internal agent whose approach to achieving objectives isn't limited by conventional rules or established ways of doing things.

Ninjas

Let's indulge in a bit of the background context to ninjas. Unlike samurai (who were born into the class, like knights in European aristocracy), ninjas were recruited from the lower classes (often as spies for the samurai). This is important. Where samurai were born to the blade (irrespective of skill), ninjas were recruited based on merit and could advance only so far as their talent took them. And because they were free from the constraints of honour, tradition and other rules, ninjas could use unconventional methods to achieve their objectives, including espionage, sabotage and other sneaky practices.

To me, the ninja epitomises the concept of moving forward with agility and guile to achieve objectives and progress change. They do not enjoy the fanfare and trumpets that usually accompany the heroes. But the work they do is non-robotic; in the modern idiom, a ninja is someone with elite skills who can get the job done.

If you say, 'I want to recruit a marketing ninja to get more people to attend our launch event', what you're really saying is, 'I want someone who can produce epic results in a short time. I don't care how they do it—it just needs to be done'.

According to data compiled by the job-listing site indeed.com, between 2006 and 2012 there was a 7000 per cent growth in the number of job listings that included the term *ninja*. Are people really looking to employ shuriken-hurling ninjas to eliminate their foes? Probably not. (And if you're looking for work I wouldn't recommend you call yourself a ninja, which would be kind of like saying, 'I'm awesome'.)

But companies are looking for specialists who can surgically remove the obstacles that stand between where they are and where they want to be.

The qualities of a ninja are very much like the qualities of rogues. Specifically, I think the three defining traits of your modern work ninja are:

- **An objective focus with agility in methodology.** Unlike samurai, ninjas aren't bound by rigid codes of honour or rules of conduct. They can happily stray from the path of bushido (in other words, the conventional way of doing things) if it means making progress and getting things done.

- **A level of earned eliteness in skill and thought.** Through expertise and experience, good ninjas are able to cut to the core of what's needed, rather than fluff around with novice activities or unnecessary procedures.

- **An ability to get the job done, and vanish without a trace.** Ninjas can be relied on to get in, get the job done and get out clean.

The world needs more ninjas.

You need to be more ninja. Right now, the world is full of robots, and the cheapest robot wins. Algorithmic/formulaic and repetitive tasks with predictable outcomes are increasingly being outsourced or automised. It's the non-robot stuff, the outside-of-the-box, innovation-ninja stuff that really counts.

Where are you, ninja?

This is probably one of the most important questions you can ask yourself these days. What is it that you do faster and better than most? And how can you keep being a ninja in your work?

CHAPTER SUMMARY

In this chapter we've seen that the path to change carries with it the inherent challenge and discomfort of uncertainty. It's hard, and there is no magical fix.

Put simply, progress is inconvenient.

To lead and drive change we need to lean into the challenge, and tackle it with motivation strategy and design — crafting the process to work. This starts by gathering a diverse team who share the aspiration for change. A clear vision needs to be captured, and this needs to be communicated vigorously. Leaders need to manage the process, and managers need to be empowered to lead.

As the world is changing fast, it's the formulaic robot-work that's most at risk from outsourcing or automation. To stay ahead of the game, we need to think more like ninjas and adapt through change, following the cleverest path of least resistance.

As Einstein once said, 'We cannot solve our problems with the same thinking we used when we created them'. Progressing through change means thinking differently.

It also means bridging the big motivation gap.

AND YET...THE BIG
MOTIVATION GAP

Genius is 1 per cent inspiration and 99 per cent perspiration.

— Thomas Edison

So far we've established that:

1. motivation is warped, and

2. stuff needs to change, but

3. change is hard.

So how do we kickstart the process of meaningful progress and change?

Constructive Discontent

'Constructive discontent' is a fancy way of describing the gap between our present state and our desired future state. This can be explained on the back of a napkin. The explanation will of course be flawed but, like most models, still useful.

Draw a circle on the left-hand side of the page (just like in figure 3.1). That's you. Or your team, or your company, or your customer. It's where things are currently at.

Now draw another circle to the right. That's where you want stuff to be.

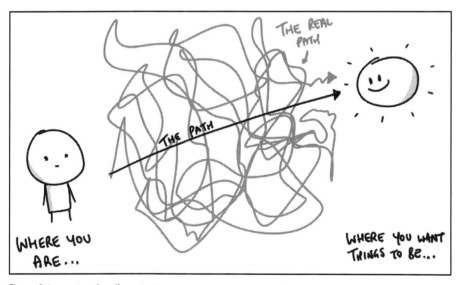

Figure 3.1: constructive discontent

It's a better place, over there. Customers buy more, and they love your stuff. Your company profits grow, and you as an individual are in a better state than you are now. Healthier, wealthier, more secure, and so on. That right-hand circle is a representation of your aspiration — of the direction you want things to head.

And now draw a line between the two dots. That's your path, your process. Your journey towards success. (Remember, of course, that success is a shifting target, and not the best thing to focus on — it's the gap that needs our attention.)

There are things that will distract and demotivate. But there are things that will support and motivate you. Some of this occurs internally, inside your head; some of it occurs externally, in the goals you set.

But what happens if you've got no gap?

If you've got no gap, then one of three things is happening.

1. You are happy and content

And good on you. You're exactly where you want to be in life. Your team is functioning and performing brilliantly. Things are secure, and there are no immediate or anticipated threats to your bliss. There's no need to do anything differently, because everything is perfect.

This is wonderful, but also a temporary state of delusion.

Why? Because things change. And contentment can easily lead to comfort, which can turn into complacency, which can then result in stagnation — and that's the second cause of 'no gap'.

Special note: Happiness is a tricky thing. When managing the gap, one can easily fall into a perpetual state of discontent. This usually happens when happiness is anchored to the achievement of a particular state, rather than the process of achieving it. We'll talk more about this distinction later in the chapter.

2. Things have stagnated

Stagnation is defined as 'the cessation of development'. It's what happens to an inactive body of water (and it encourages parasites to breed). It's the erosion of aspiration. When things have stagnated, there is no growth, and no change. Rather than the temporary blissful delusion provided by contentedness, stagnation can become a much more fixed state of despondency.

At times like these, things need to change. Desperately.

It's in this situation that many organisations will jump to desperately ambitious stretch goals. Professor Sim Sitkin, of Duke University's Fuqua School of Business, completed a study of such goals, and found they were most likely to be pursued by desperate, embattled companies that would have difficulty adapting if the goals failed.

3. You're in automation mode

You've got your systems and routines down pat. Things are running smoothly—you're busy, but not challenged. You don't need to think so much; you just need to do what you do. The thinking has already been done, and the systems are working. Just do your job.

Naturally, this one's a delusion too. But to change the game, shift motivation and make progress happen, we need to shift from automation to aspiration. And that means something's gotta change...

From automation to aspiration

If you've ever wondered why someone isn't motivated to do something, or why people aren't enthusiastic about change, it might be that they aren't yet aspiring to do it. When it comes to influencing motivation and behaviour, everything works better if you can get this bit right. Figure 3.2 shows a model that explains this process.

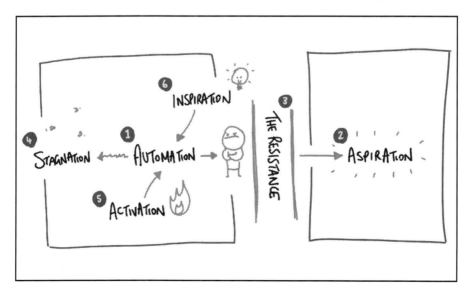

Figure 3.2: from automation to aspiration

As shown in the model, it starts with *automation* (1). Automation left unchecked can lead to *stagnation* (4). To convert automation to *aspiration* (2), we need *inspiration* (6) or some sort of *activation* (5) — and these factors need to be powerful enough to overcome the inherent *resistance* (3) and inertia.

Let's look at each in a bit more detail.

1. Automation — the thing we default to

Most of us are, by default, in automation mode. We are pattern-seeking animals, and there is immense comfort in the familiar. As previously discussed, established systems help to preserve our energy and attention. Things are easier. The cognitive (and emotional) burden of trying to figure out what needs to be done, when, and by whom, is minimal.

Automation is a good state to be in, when it's working. We simply cannot maintain high levels of motivation to drive change at all times, so having a structure to keep things humming along is a good thing.

Automation is not so good, however, when it gets in the way of agility and improvement, when habits become so ingrained that they become a stubbornness to change. Sometimes automation leads to non-thinking complacency, which can lead to stagnation and an inability to respond to change.

In today's business environment, we need to be clever with how we automate our systems and processes — to keep them fixed enough to work but adaptable enough to grow. It's a paradox, for sure. Changing the game when systems are broken, or when there are pressing economic, social or environmental pressures — ah, that's easier.

But changing the game when systems are running fine — that's where things get harder. It's here we need to be inspired to change, or to have circumstances activate the need for it.

2. Inspiration — the internal precursor

Sometimes we can proactively create the stimulus for change by tapping into, or crafting, inspiration on what's possible. And, while brainstorming has been shown to be fairly ineffective at generating good ideas (let alone inspiration), a good workshop, conference or meeting, or anything that exposes you to diverse perspectives on what's possible, can facilitate the inspiration that leads to breakthrough thinking.

Inspiration is defined as 'the process of being mentally stimulated to do or feel something, especially to do something creative'. Most innovation, improvement and change comes from individuals and teams thinking differently about challenges and opportunities. This creative thinking is usually assisted by exposure to new ideas and conversations in new contexts, allowing people to connect disparate pieces of inspiration or to view possibilities from new perspectives.

It can be an incredibly powerful thing, and is the precursor to aspiration. But, as we know from previous chapters, inspiration is a fickle thing. Authors Jason Fried and David Heinemeier describe inspiration as akin to milk, in that it expires. Organisations and teams can binge on inspiration at kick-off events and sales conferences, but inevitably the reality hangover awaits as we face up to the resistance.

If we're going to seek inspiration, we need to be sure we are not simply seeking entertainment or excitement, but rather something more useful.

HOW TO GET USEFULLY INSPIRED

Here are a few practical things you can do to stimulate better thinking at work.

Attend a good conference or event

For inspiration, look outside your industry and find an event that has a focus on future thinking. If you do attend an event from your own industry, meet and connect with new people, and maximise the gaps between sessions to engage in the types of conversations you would otherwise not get the chance to have at work.

Host an informal TED meeting

TED, a phenomenal conference on technology, entertainment and design, is all about 'ideas worth spreading'. The stories and insights shared on TED are among the most profound in the world—and you can access them at www.ted.com—all for free.

A few of my clients have begun to incorporate TED talks into their monthly staff meetings. Each month a different staff member will nominate a TED talk (it can be on any topic — from creativity to vulnerability, the human brain to giant squids), along with a thought-provoking question to stimulate good thinking and conversation. This can revolutionise what may otherwise be a very stale routine, and given how contextually relevant it often is, this ritual can trigger new inspiration at work.

Run an internal PechaKucha event

PechaKucha, Japanese for 'chit-chat', is a dynamic presentation format in which presenters share 20 slides, each automatically shown for 20 seconds (making for a total presentation length of six minutes and 40 seconds). The format keeps presentations concise, light and fast-paced. In 90 minutes, you can get through at least half a dozen presentations, including time for questions and facilitation.

Why would you want to do this? Done once per quarter, a PechaKucha event can be a great way to harvest new ideas from people. Depending upon the contextual theme established, staff can contribute thoughts and ideas, or simply expose co-workers to new things they may not have heard of or seen before. This serves to stimulate thinking, which can trigger new inspiration for change.

One of my clients now hosts a quarterly event that mixes live PechaKucha presentations on 'micro-innovations' — little improvements, ideas and developments that enhance efficiency and value. These are harvested from within the organisation, irrespective of hierarchy, and serve to foster, anchor and amplify the types of behaviours they want to see more of. You get what you focus on, and this ritual has been incorporated into a broader cultural alignment strategy.

These events are recorded for their internal network. People who are unable to attend can to submit short three-minute smartphone videos to be screened at the event. This, again, is deliberate. By removing the need to create 'perfect' videos on professional equipment, much of the friction for participation is removed.

3. Activation—the external precursor

On the flip side to inspiring change, sometimes we are activated into aspiration in reaction to external changes. To put it proverbially: shit gets real, and what we end up with is a 'burning platform'.

In the lead-up to Apple's first iPhone release, there was a limited opportunity to be first to market for different accessory items (such as cases and covers). Manufacturers and design teams had only rumours to run with, but the opportunity to tap into a big, enthusiastic market was just too great for many to ignore. That's an example of externally activated aspiration.

But activation is not usually a positive opportunity. Usually, it's a looming or imminent threat.

One of my clients is a multinational pharmaceutical company that makes 'generic' patent-free drugs and medications with market demand. It's traditionally a conservative industry, but regulatory shifts, along with changing cost structures in manufacturing, mean that the leaders in countries like Australia (where manufacturing is relatively expensive) need to change, lest their global competitors win out.

All of these things can activate a dramatic need to innovate; it's almost an 'innovate or die' scenario. Stagnation is what happens when there is no investment in innovation, improvement or progress.

4. Stagnation—the thing we want to avoid

Stagnation is what occurs when people persist, oblivious to change, when there's no inspiration to do better or when 'the resistance' outweighs any activation elements.

Organisations and teams in stagnation present a real challenge. By now, negative or dysfunctional behaviours have become normalised, and there is a tendency to feel powerless, a sense that the system is too big and people too set in their ways to change. There will also be enhanced pessimism towards conventional forms of inspiration.

When in stagnation, much work needs to be done in co-crafting and communicating the purpose and vision for the organisation first, as outlined in chapter 2.

5. Resistance—the thing we need to overcome

This is the threshold one needs to cross, and the first battle is an internal one. What you're up against: inconvenience, failure, unrecognised and unrewarded effort, difficulty, risk, and so on. Suspended disbelief can sometimes help us outwit the resistance and progress towards aspiration, but ultimately we need to keep things pragmatic. And this often comes down to a simple assessment—is it worth it?

Is this change, this desired new state, worth the effort, risk and inconvenience required to achieve it? It's usually here that inspiration collapses. Those 'big hairy audacious goals' we're told to set usually end up confronting a harsh reality: to make this stuff happen takes work (it's the not-so-secret secret to all progress and success).

So is the solution to avoid big audacious goals and risk? Heck no! It's about making the harsh reality of progress *less* harsh and more blissful. We need to be more agile and ninja-like, to sneak past, circumvent or outwit the resistance.

6. Aspiration—the precursor to motivation and progress

Inspiration and aspiration may sound similar, but they are two very different concepts. If we manage to convert inspiration to aspiration, we're on the path to motivation and changing the game. **Inspiration is about emotion**. It's how we feel mentally stimulated to do, or feel, something. **Aspiration is about ambition**. It's what we have when we are aiming to achieve a particular goal.

Aspiration is asymptotic: you are always short of reaching the point you aspire to, because once you succeed in reaching it, it will no longer be an aspiration.

Aspiration can also be a result of inspiration, and can change under the influence of a strong inspiration. Inspiration, therefore, plays a critical role in triggering the need to think differently.

Once we have aspiration—whether from inspiration or activation—we have a constructive discrepancy between where we are and where we want to be. In essence, *we have a gap.*

Bridging the gap

Got aspiration? Good. Let's come back to the gap. I've redrawn it for you here in figure 3.3.

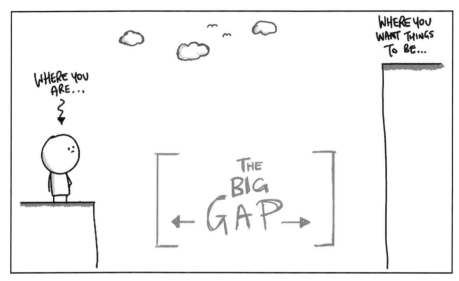

Figure 3.3: the big motivation gap

We've covered a bit of ground here, but just so we're clear: it's all about the gap. All motivation, progress, growth, development and change lives within this gap.

Before we get carried away, a note on intrinsic and extrinsic motivation

You've probably heard these two terms bandied around, but let's do a quick summary.

Intrinsic (or inherent) motivation

A person motivated in this way undertakes an activity for its own sake, for the enjoyment it provides, the learning, development and growth it permits, or the feeling of accomplishment it creates.

When people are intrinsically motivated, they're more likely to give careful attention to what they are doing, maintaining a careful awareness of the complexities, inconsistencies and integrations associated with an activity. In other words, they are more likely to be 'immersed' in the activity.

The rewards of intrinsic motivation come from the activity itself, rather than from the result of the activity. In other words, the activity is the reward—it is *inherently* motivating.

I have learned to substitute the term *inherent motivation* for intrinsic motivation, as many people confuse intrinsic motivation with *internal* factors such as values, beliefs, attitudes, goals, vision and alignment. This is a vague, messy mix of elements, and unless you have a lot of time and a very sophisticated approach, it is largely a distraction.

Many of the 'internal' motivational issues in people's heads and hearts can be fixed with good work design—making activities that are inherently motivating, aligned with purpose and geared for progress.

Extrinsic (or external) motivation

Extrinsically motivated behaviour is undertaken to obtain a reward or outcome, or to avoid punishment. What you are seeking to obtain or avoid is usually unrelated to the activity; therefore the motivation doesn't come from within you, or from within the task itself—it comes from outside.

The lines between intrinsic, internal and extrinsic motivation can sometimes be blurred. For example, praise from your boss may be a form of extrinsic motivation—if you are motivated to complete a task simply for praise and recognition. However, it can also be a form of intrinsic/inherent motivation—if you are motivated to complete the task for the progress it brings, then praise may be a form of feedback that informs further progress.

The danger of relying on extrinsic motivation elements is that they can displace the inherent motivation within activities. In essence, extrinsic motivators can muddy the waters of intrinsic motivation, making it harder to connect with the inherent motivation of an activity. By adding an extrinsic motivator like an incentive or a reward to a task, what you are essentially communicating is: 'This task is so inherently unmotivating that I need to motivate you with a reward'.

We will unpack some of the dangers of rewards (and goals) in this chapter, but do note, it's not all bad. And it's certainly not a case of extrinsic versus intrinsic or inherent motivation. Real professionals in work design know that we need to take and combine the best elements of both worlds to craft the games that drive progress at work.

The classic (internal) motivational approach

Internal motivation is represented on the left side of figure 3.3 on p. 56 (inside the character's head and heart). It's where things like attitudes, values and beliefs live.

I remember one guy giving a motivational presentation to a bunch of final-year students. He opened by saying they need a 'check-up from the neck up', and that the source of all of their motivational challenges stems from a poor attitude. In fact, I think his talk was titled something like 'A Kick Up the Attitude'.

Anyway, you're probably picking up a vibe from me here. The issue with motivation, in most cases, is not to do with attitude. That type of approach can only ever come off as patronising.

But we do tend to overemphasise the stuff that happens inside people's heads. Is it powerful? Yes, very. But can we change it? Not without a whole heap of sophisticated and individualised effort.

Forgive me for harping on a bit, but the motivation world is rife with well-intended yet scientifically invalid fluff. Stuff that'll waste your time and, in many cases, *reduce* your (and your team's) motivation.

Positive fantasies make your goals less likely to come true.

'Think positively and visualise your success' — this is a classic, internally focused approach to enhancing motivation. It's an oft-used throwaway line from the old-school motivational toolkit. Just visualise having achieved your goal. Simple, right?

The trouble is, a good amount of research now shows that indulging in positive fantasies makes your or your team's aspirations less likely to become reality. Why? Because mentally indulging in a desired future has been shown to sap your energy.

In an article in the *Journal of Experimental Social Psychology*, researchers Dr Heather Kappes and Professor Gabriele Oettingen from New York University and the University of Hamburg explain that the classic activity of visualising success makes the energy required to achieve them seem unnecessary. We effectively trick ourselves into believing we have already attained our goal.

Just like depression could be an adaptive mechanism to protect us from blind optimism, an internal trigger that reduces the perceived need to invest energy could be viewed as another survival mechanism to protect us from pursuing the unobtainable.

So what should we do instead?

'Fantasies that are less positive—that question whether an ideal future can be achieved, and that depict obstacles, problems and setbacks—should be more beneficial for mustering the energy needed to obtain success', the researchers argue. In other words, get pragmatic and focus on tackling the challenges at hand—the stuff that will give you *the clearest sense of progress*.

Similar studies published in *Psychological Science* have found that repeating positive mantras about themselves ('I can do it! I'm a successful person') makes people with lower self-esteem feel worse.

If you're leading teams, please do yourself and everyone a favour and don't ever say, 'You can do it, team! You each have so much potential. Just stay focused, stay positive, and amazing things will happen!'

It's just a bunch of useless hot air. You're more likely to get significant motivation wins by being pragmatic and working with the challenge, rather than by simply 'being positive'.

We need to focus on *progress*, not success.

Progress, not success. (See what I did there? I made it a mantra. But this one is an effective one, you'll see. More on that soon.)

Progress trumps success any day of the week.

Don't get me wrong, the internal stuff is incredibly powerful when approached with a sophisticated methodology. That's why coaching is such an effective intervention, if the coach knows what they are doing.

But that's hard to do on a scale larger than 1:1, and it takes a lot of effort to implement and sustain. So we should switch to the external factors that influence motivation, right?

The conventional (extrinsic) management approach

Set goals and offer rewards. That's what old-school management typically does if given half the chance. And the thing is, like goal setting, it works to focus attention. Dramatically well...

...over a short time frame and for very specific behaviours. And that's exactly the point.

The world of work we are moving to requires more ninjas (creative, agile and knowledgeable workers with skills machines can't replicate). The routine, formulaic work *does* benefit greatly from the narrow focus of rewards. But these tasks don't happen in a vacuum.

Don't get me wrong—goals and rewards definitely do work; but they can work *too* well, and backfire tremendously.

Is goal setting the solution?

Goal setting tends to be the 'serious' person's panacea for motivation. I've seen teachers teach it in schools, and a few of my multinational clients have their global HR departments training the whole organisation in SMART (specific, measurable, achievable, relevant, time-based) goal setting as part of their performance reviews. This is often done in the belief that it will enhance the motivation required to achieve things.

And it does, to an extent, but only if the work is formulaic and routine, with predictable outcomes. The clarity and structure will help people to see progress (which is incredibly motivating). So, if you've got a heap of data to crunch, some boxes to pack or a marathon to train for, goal setting can be great. It consolidates your aspiration and fires up your intention to engage in the activities that will help you achieve your goals.

Goal setting has become such an unquestioned and embedded practice in organisations. Why? Because there's a heap of clinical evidence to support it, it's easy to implement, and it's easy to measure and document success.

But, as Professor Ayelet Fishbach and Dr Jinhee Choi point out, focusing on goals detracts from the inherent pleasures of the activities we need to pursue in order to achieve those goals. There's that word again—*inherent*.

When goal setting goes wrong

In their article, published in *Organizational Behavior and Human Decision Processes*, Fishbach and Choi found that by focusing on external factors like the ultimate goal of an activity, we risk destroying the inherent motivation of the activity itself. (Yes, that's right—it's not just rewards that can muddle and displace inherent motivation; goals can do it too.)

Building from this, psychologist Dr Christian Jarrett argues: 'Revel in the process and you're more likely to make it to the finishing line.' You can probably tell by now that we're building to something. But let's look at a few more external factors.

Managers often default to goal setting because they seem to have no better option. Key performance indicators are linked to goal performance, and the main way to 'engage' employees in work that can't otherwise be mandated is to encourage them to set aspirational development and contribution goals as part of their mandatory performance reviews. The clients that have engaged me for motivation strategy and design usually have some sort of system like this to start with. At best, it's a well-intended yet shallow, tokenistic, one-size-fits-all approach to performance at work. At worst, goal performance is linked to incentivised targets that cripple creativity and collaboration, creating an overly narrow focus that neglects non-goal areas and increases the likelihood of unethical behaviour, distorted risk preferences, and the corrosion of creativity, collaboration and culture.

Here's one example of how goals can narrow thinking: the Ford Pinto. Presented with a goal to build a car 'under 2000 pounds and under $2000', by 1970, employees overlooked safety testing and designed a car where the petrol tank was vulnerable to explosion from rear-end collisions. Fifty-three people died as a result.

In another example, human resources expert Susan Heathfield establishes that organisations often fail to achieve goals and strategic planning targets that are set top down by executives who lack crucial information and are out of touch with staff challenges. The goals, Heathfield argues, are unrealistic and fail to consider resources and capabilities. Staff members don't believe that the rewards they will receive for accomplishing goals will equal the energy they invest to achieve them. And frequently managers are intimidated when they fear job loss for failure.

Heathfield recounts the story of a former executive at a large IT firm: 'My favorite goal setting story of all time was how [the company] set sales goals for its District Managers: everyone's quota was $3.5 million. There, no more thought needed to go into it, no discussion—just do it or you're fired!' The executive recounted how he would spend the last day of every sales quarter performing 'unnatural acts' to close business and save his job. 'At the end of the year, I had to work until 10.00 pm on the last day of the sales quarter (while we had company over at home) to get one last deal closed. This deal saved my job.' He was one of the two regional sales executives who avoided being fired two weeks later.

I've worked with executives in a large multinational enterprise software company that features a similar 'quarterly sales focus'. All executive staff still need to hit sales goals. 'Two bad quarters and you're out' is the understanding across the organisation. Naturally, this has devastating implications for mid- to long-term strategic planning and innovation.

Management Professor Adam Galinsky, co-author of a Harvard Business School report titled 'Goals Gone Wild', argues that 'goal setting has been treated like an over-the-counter medication when it should really be treated with more care, as a prescription-strength medication'. He argues that goal setting can focus attention too much or on the wrong things, and can lead people to participate in extreme behaviours to achieve the goals.

Professor Maurice Schweitzer of the University of Pennsylvania and Professor Lisa Ordonez of the University of Arizona both studied the psychology of goal attainment. Several of their experiments have shown that when people self-reported the achievement of their goals, a significant percentage of them lied in order to make up for any shortcomings in their results.

This could be because goal setting can create anxiety and fear associated with goals. Leadership expert Ray Williams surmises that there are psychological manifestations associated with not achieving goals that may be more damaging than not having any goals at all. As we've seen before, the process of goal setting—in teams and individually—can establish desires that are removed from everyday reality.

Highly aspirational goals require us to develop new competencies, some of which may be beyond our current capabilities. As we develop these competencies, we are likely to experience failures, which then become de-motivational if the process is poorly designed (more on this soon). Also, goal setting can establish an either/or polarity of success. 'The only true measure can either be 100 per cent attainment or perfection, or 99 per cent and less, which is failure', Williams argues. We then often focus only on the few missing or incomplete elements of our efforts, ignoring the successful parts. And finally, goal setting doesn't take into account all of the variables that may influence success—some things are just beyond our control.

Now, remember—I used to be in this camp. A large part of my doctoral research hinged on behavioural interventions that incorporated goal setting as a key motivational tactic. I taught at universities, spoke at schools and worked with businesses sharing the research on goal setting, and there are a lot of positive elements to it. But increasingly it is overemphasised, and it just doesn't work in isolation. Goals need to be combined with other elements, and used with extreme caution.

One of my clients works at a large research and development branch for a multinational fast manufactured consumable goods organisation. His team is responsible for the product innovations that ultimately can disrupt markets and drive growth. And yet, he lamented to me, his research team is still mandated to stick to protracted SMART goals and rigid, distal key performance indicators. And so he—like many others in a similar position—precariously dances around mandated goals and performance measures, effectively gaming the system so that the real progress-making work can get done.

Work, particularly knowledge work like this, requires a certain amount of creativity and judgement. Collapsing complex activities into a set of goal numbers (set into the future) can end up derailing progress and rewarding the wrong behaviours.

I once made a post (in my popular 'making clever happen' museletter) about how 'smart goal setting is dumb for motivation'. It was met with a lot of positive responses, but a few of the life coaches and business coaches subscribed to the museletter were vehemently loathing in reply to this. It was as if I had ruffled the feathers of their god or something.

Goal setting is so firmly enmeshed in the motivational and managerial folklore that guides a lot of decisions today, and many have invested a lot into the process. It's become part of their core belief system as well as an integral part of their core methodology. And people can get mighty defensive when goal setting is scrutinised.

Sometimes this love of goal setting can get in the way of the *doing the work required to progress and achieve the goal* bit. You know, the '99 per cent perspiration' component. It is a serious downside when 'the ratio of energy, time and creativity that goes into creating the goal outstrips the effort required to actually manage the project', as HR expert Susan Heathfield observes.

Professor Laura King and Professor Chad Burton of the University of Missouri wrote an article for the American Psychological Association titled 'The Hazards of Goal Pursuit'. They argue that goals should be used only in the narrowest of circumstances: 'The optimally striving individual ought to endeavour to achieve and approach goals that only slightly implicate the self; that are only moderately important, fairly easy, and moderately abstract; that do not conflict with each other, and that concern the accomplishment of something other than financial gain.'

A new approach

Finally, Professor Max Bazerman from the Harvard Business School argues that, rather than relying on goals, we should create workplaces and schools that foster interest in and a passion for work. Research shows that an even stronger effect than goals is *intrinsic* motivation — having individuals do an activity because they find the work, progress and change inherently rewarding.

And that, dear chap (or chapess), is one of the key premises of this book.

As will soon be revealed, goals are but one of the three main components of good game design. There is at least one other component that's even more important. And later, in Part III, we'll be unpacking a better way to approach goal setting — specifically contextual momentum with missions and quests.

But let's cast our eyes over the other element of extrinsic motivation—the big one. Rewards. And the thing to get right before it: hygiene.

Herzberg's hygiene factors

Frederick Herzberg, one of the most influential management consultants and professors of the modern postwar era, is probably best known for his challenging thinking on work and motivation. In 1959 Herzberg wrote that 'the factors which motivate people at work are different to and not simply the opposite of the factors which cause dissatisfaction'.

The way Herzberg saw it, a decent salary was simply one of the many hygiene (or 'maintenance') factors required to enable good work. Just as soap is important if you haven't washed in a while, money is important if your base needs and reasonable aspirations aren't being met. But then, just as more soap isn't all that useful if you're clean, more money is nice but not reliable as a motivator if base needs are already being met (see figure 3.4).

Figure 3.4: money is a threshold motivator

Don't get me wrong, money is still a very powerful extrinsic motivator.

But—and it's a big 'but'—money is only a threshold motivator. It's powerful only up to a certain point, then its effectiveness plateaus and other things become more important.

This threshold will be different for everyone, and will depend upon their current context. If you've got a mortgage to pay and a family to support, you're going to need money to cover these things.

And if you are weighing up two different job opportunities, you'll give more weight to quantitative rationalising over qualitative reasoning—a higher base pay is easier to rationalise than more diverse and creative challenges.

Perhaps Derek Sivers, the founder and former president of CD Baby, sums it up best. People have to earn a living—salary and some benefits and perks are what he calls 'baseline rewards'. If someone's baseline rewards aren't fair or adequate, their focus will be on the unfairness of the situation (and the anxiety that comes from it). Here, Sivers argues, 'you'll get neither the predictability of extrinsic motivation, nor the weirdness of intrinsic motivation. You'll get very little motivation at all'.

Once we are past this threshold, Sivers argues, the classic 'carrots and sticks' approach can achieve the exact opposite of its intended aims. He adds:

> Mechanisms designed to increase motivation can dampen it. Tactics aimed at boosting creativity can reduce it. Programs to promote good deeds can make them disappear. Meanwhile, instead of restraining negative behaviour, rewards and punishments can often set it loose—and give rise to cheating, addiction, and dangerously myopic thinking.

The key for any employer is to get money out of the equation early.

Pay well, provide a good base package, and then focus on the motivational opportunities inherent within the work (which is the premise of this book). Use incentives and rewards cautiously for short sprints of grunt work, and use good motivation design to bring out the best in your team.

Now, just take all of the bad points about goals, and dial them up a notch with rewards

Rewards act like mini-goals. They narrow focus, cripple creativity, distort risk assessment and can influence people to act in unethical ways or to engage in behaviours not aligned with the bigger purpose.

Imagine this: you have a teacher who does an amazing job at inspiring real learning from her students. Perhaps you can remember an awesome teacher you had when you were young.

This teacher goes beyond the call of duty. She is innovative, her students love her classes, and she shares her resources liberally with other teachers, parents and the school. And she is not alone—there is a great collegiality among the staff and a general bias towards collaboration.

The new principal wants to see more of this happening in his school, and he thinks that brilliant work like this should not go unrewarded. Using our hero teacher as the shining example, he introduces a new reward scheme: 'The top 10 per cent of teachers will be given a $10 000 bonus at the end of the year', he boldly proclaims.

There are 40 teaching staff at this school. And now they start eyeing each other off, wondering who will be in the top four to receive the reward; $10 000 is a lot of money, after all.

Activities begin to narrow. Teachers who would otherwise innovate and think creatively now perform within the parameters dictated by the reward. Those teachers who used to share their resources have stopped collaborating; things have got competitive.

And then the bickering and politics start—and what was once a wonderful culture of collaboration focused on enhancing learning opportunities for students has now become a bitter culture of compliance and competition. People view some teachers as clearly 'favourites' of the principal, and ultimately it's the students that suffer—no teacher is going to waste effort on anything that may not help them to achieve the reward. (Of course, the good teachers would. I have done a lot of work with teachers, and one thing's for sure: they are motivated by much more than incentives and renumeration.)

Hopefully this example serves to illustrate the effect a well-intended external intervention can have on the motivational dynamics within a work culture.

By Pavlov's salivating dogs!

While this sounds like an obscure pirate curse, you probably know the story of Ivan Pavlov, a Russian researcher born in 1849. In 1904 he won the Nobel Prize for Medicine for his research into dog saliva. He measured the amount of saliva a dog produces as the start of digestion. He noticed that dogs began to salivate before they started eating.

He also noticed that some dogs began to salivate as soon as they saw the food, and some salivated even before they saw the food. He determined that salivation could be triggered by something the dogs associated with food, such as the smell of food, footsteps down the hall or the ringing of a bell. These things were cues and triggers that indicated to the dogs that food was about to arrive.

Pavlov called this *classical conditioning*. In a nutshell, it works like this: a stimulus is provided (the smell of food), followed by a trigger to activate the response (footsteps or the bell ringing).

It is Pavlov's classical conditioning that forms the basis of more conventional thinking about rewards, which holds that if you create conditions where people expect rewards, then you are more likely to get the behaviour you want.

People are not dogs, however. Nor are we rats—although we occasionally demonstrate similar behaviours.

Take casinos or poker machines, for example. Both vary the reward rate—it's called the *variable ratio reward*—because people are more likely to invest their effort and remain engaged if they are uncertain of what they are going to get.

As a game, *World of Warcraft* use this tactic extremely well. Sometimes you are rewarded with a rare magical item, but you never know when that might happen. So you keep playing in hope of scoring a rare item. There is no way to predict it.

Poker machines use the same tactic, only they use complex algorithms that allow people to feel like they almost win. This keeps them further engaged despite less reward being delivered.

This incredibly powerful method of motivation stems from research by B. F. Skinner. Rather than focusing on stimulus and response, Skinner used rats and pigeons to experiment on how rewards influence behaviour. This is called *operant conditioning*, as opposed to Pavlov's classical conditioning.

Skinner redefined rewards as reinforcements. What he determined was that instead of providing a fixed schedule of rewards, a variable ratio had a much more powerful effect on the rats' behaviour.

Skinner's five basic schedules of reinforcement are the result of his experiments. The same schedules now inform gamification initiatives and other rewards programs. If the tasks being rewarded are routine, formulaic ones, variable rate rewards work well. For more complex tasks, however, something much more sophisticated is needed.

Skinner's five schedules of reinforcement

Here are the five main reinforcement/reward schedules Skinner identified. Please don't interpret this as me advocating a pure, rewards-based approach to motivation. This type of operant conditioning may work on rats, but human and ninja work is more complex, and requires a much more sophisticated approach. Still, it's important you're aware of the effect variability of scheduling and ratios can have on the efficacy of rewards.

Continuous reinforcement

In this experiment, Skinner provided food every time the rat pressed a bar. The equivalent real-world example is praising staff every time they hand in a report on time. By doing this, you are setting up a continuous reinforcement schedule: report on time = praise.

It's useful to get people to do new things but, over time, it loses its effectiveness.

Fixed interval reinforcement

In this experiment, Skinner provided food only after a fixed interval of time had passed. The rat would get food the first time it pressed the bar after a five-minute interval. If the rat pressed the bar before the five minutes was up, no food would appear.

This is the least effective reward method; but because it is so easy to understand and implement, it happens to be the most common. Performance reviews and bonuses are paid once a year — it's a known, fixed interval! Once people expect it, it has no effect on their behaviour except when they know that it counts — just before bonus time!

Variable interval reinforcement

Skinner also experimented with providing rats with food after variable time periods. Sometimes it was one minute later, other times five, and yet others ten minutes.

Variable intervals establish stable behaviour. When the goal is to have people do something regularly but not often, a variable interval schedule works. For example, if employees are in diverse locations, you make occasional, unscheduled visits at variable times to check everything is fine. This is more likely to produce a good average level of stability rather than a rush in behaviours prior to a regular, pre-planned visit.

Fixed ratio reinforcement

Skinner also experimented with fixed ratios where, instead of basing reinforcement on time, he based it on the number of times the rat pressed the bar. The rat would get food after ten bar presses. This resulted in a burst of behaviour.

This is what coffee loyalty cards are based on. For every ten coffees you buy, you get one free! As a coffee snob, I feel that cafes that resort to such tactics are kidding themselves about customer loyalty. The only sure way to earn loyalty is to make amazing coffee.

With fixed ratios, people are more motivated the closer they get to a goal. If you have only two stamps and you need another eight to 'get one free', you're not really that motivated. But when you're up to number eight or nine, your motivation increases!

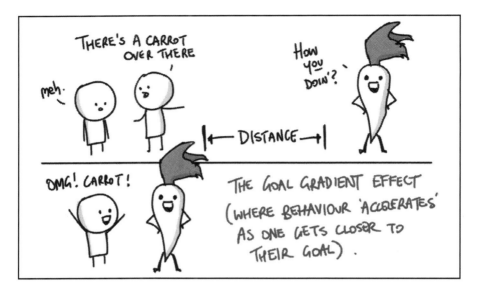

This is called the *goal-gradient effect*. It was first studied in 1934 by Clark Hull, who found that people will accelerate their behaviour as they progress closer to a goal.

I think of this as bias towards completion. Rather than someone else fixing the intervals, you can create your own sense of progress around important tasks, then you can narrow the distance between where you are and where you want to be. You can tap into your own goal-gradient effect!

Variable ratio reinforcement

This form of reinforcement was based on the number of bar presses, but the number required to get food varied. This is the most effective type of reinforcement reward system, it keeps people doing the same things, over and over.

It's the poker machine scenario I was discussing earlier. If a player wins at a poker machine after playing 56 rounds, that's a variable schedule. Yet, if the player at the next machine wins a reward after only a few rounds, it's incredibly frustrating for the longer-term player. The only thing that people do in this instance is keep playing!

Out of all the reward schedules, this is the most manipulative. Psychologists argue that this behaviour is 'resistant to extinction'. After a long period of time, even if the rewards are removed the behaviour persists. That is, if you set up this reward framework, and people participate and experience levels of reward, it is very powerful in creating repetitive behaviour — to a point where it can be a problem. It's a schedule that should be treated with caution. Remember, people are not rats and they usually work out what's going on.

So, if you are looking to harness the power of intelligent people doing ninja work, then you need to keep things authentic and transparent, moving beyond fixed reward schedules. And let's remember: rewards are secondary to our work in making the process inherently motivating.

We're in a time of massive transition. Our understanding of what really motivates us has evolved, and now some businesses are catching up.

HOW TO MAKE REWARDS WORK — A GUIDE FOR BUSY MANAGERS

I've worked with Darren Hill, a behavioural scientist and co-author of *Dealing with the Tough Stuff*, on motivation strategies and culture change programs in large enterprises.

One of the common challenges for managers who want to shift culture and change behaviours is that they do not have the authorisation to make large structural changes to the organisation. Also, most are working in an environment where people are expected to do more with less rather than focus on fundamental organisational change.

To tackle this situation, Darren and I developed a rewards table for one of our big clients. And it's something you can put together too.

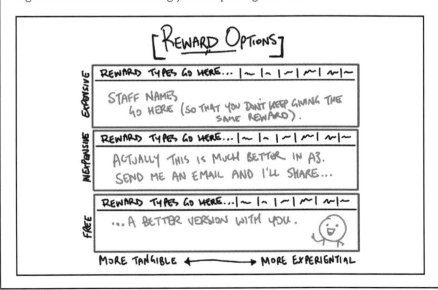

(continued)

HOW TO MAKE REWARDS WORK — A GUIDE FOR BUSY MANAGERS *cont'd*

This structure will allow you to recognise and reward good behaviour and achievement wherever relevant — that is, not at fixed times throughout the year. You'll be able to move from an 'if-you-do-this-then-you'll-get-this' extrinsic, contingent-based reward system to a 'now-that-you've-done-this-here's-this' non-contingent system.

The last thing you want to become is the 'movie voucher guy' or 'wine gift girl' type of team leader. And so I'm going to show you how you can establish your own rewards table to avoid just that, and to ensure your reinforcements are meaningful and conducive to progress.

This works even for managers who are really busy. Let's face it, all managers are busy. When we are busy we tend to default to the structures we know. Yet, if we reduce the level of thought put into this, it will diminish the effect of the reward.

Here are some fundamentals to consider when crafting a rewards table.

How much budget do you have?

Your rewards table includes things that are more expensive and things that are inexpensive. This could cover anything from gold bullion or a Rolex watch to an iPad or a voucher to attend a conference. Or even just a coffee and cupcake the next time you get a moment.

I've worked with one organisation that occasionally, spontaneously, rewards people with a ticket to a TED conference. It's expensive, amazing, unexpected and — you guessed it — very effective.

At the other end of the scale, I've worked with companies that provide small gifts, books or cards, or even telephone the person's partner to tell them how wonderful the recipient is. All these are also very effective.

The rewards table will help you keep track of the type of reward you have given each person. This way, you're not giving the same type of reward to the same person, over and over. I call this *structured authenticity*. Establishing the rewards table requires some thought, but it reduces your time spent creating a structure.

In short, it makes is easy to be authentic and reward people well.

The tangibility of rewards

Often, intangible rewards are more effective than tangible ones. If you can't convert the reward into a dollar value, the result is better.

If someone works for 20 hours across a weekend and is rewarded with a $60 bottle of wine, the maths behind the effort versus reward is simple. All that effort for $3 an hour. On a weekend.

While it's a nice gesture, being able to translate the reward into a dollar value has diminished its effect. In this instance, an intangible reward would be more effective.

Intangible benefits include allowing time to work on a pet project, offering a position in a new, interesting project, arranging access to personal mentoring, or presenting conference tickets or an experimental gift voucher.

Also consider providing time off in lieu or taking them out to lunch, perhaps with a senior boss along so you can talk up the great work they are doing.

These things are more recognition than reward. This is why they work. You're showing that you understand their contribution and that you really appreciate it.

Keep intangible recognition real and it will work. Like the First Annual Montgomery Burns Award for the Outstanding Achievement in the Field of Excellence.

Choose rewards that appeal to the individual

Choose a reward or recognition that appeals to the individual. Are they an extrovert or an introvert? This is vitally important if you're to keep the rewards authentic and personal.

Don't take your raging introvert out to lunch at a noisy restaurant followed by karaoke. A swaggering extrovert might really enjoy that reward, while the introvert might just prefer a nice quiet lunch. With cupcakes.

Make the rewards table work for you

When you assess each of these strategies in the rewards table, ensure you put them through the *recipient's* filter, not your own. Not everyone is going to enjoy a flamenco dancing class!

(continued)

HOW TO MAKE REWARDS WORK — A GUIDE FOR BUSY MANAGERS *cont'd*

A manager who, despite being busy, takes the time to recognise staff in a meaningful way will have the greatest effect.

Remember these three things:

- Don't be tokenistic. Be sincere in your intent and match the reward to the person.

- Good intention, poorly executed, diminishes motivation, loyalty and engagement.

- Don't be predictable. Variable rewards at variable intervals are the most effective.

Having said that...

I will add that sometimes it works to provide a reward that reflects something you are passionate about. It's how you go about it that matters.

I am an extreme coffee snob. The depth of my coffee knowledge is immense. Abyss-level deep. Really.

If I were to reward someone and I knew they liked coffee, I might get them a special Japanese cold-drip water brew coffee maker. It's brilliant for summer. I would also get some freshly roasted single-origin beans that I would think matched their tastes.

While their appreciation would not rely on their being a coffee snob, they would know that I had put thought into the gift and was sharing my passion with them. How I framed the gift and explained why I chose the beans and the coffee maker would show my genuine intent to provide a reward that was personal.

If you love origami, crocheting or something quirky, giving a gift that you have created can be very powerful, in the right circumstances.

It's how you frame such rewards that matters. These types of rewards can contribute to the authenticity and diversity within a work culture, which in itself can encourage positive behavioural changes.

I've said this, and I'll say it again — rewards are a secondary consideration to the activity itself. We are in the midst of a big shift in how we view and approach motivation at work, moving from payment-based motivation (extrinsic, contingent-based reward mechanisms born out of the factory era) to a more purpose-based motivation (intrinsic and non-contingent, where the work itself is the reward).

It all comes back to the gap

The most overlooked component of motivation is not the internal stuff, nor is it the extrinsic stuff like goals and rewards. It's the stuff that exists *between* where we are and where we want things to be. The stuff that exists in the gap — the work.

Taking what we know from the science of motivation, the next chapter will look at the single most effective thing you can do to unlock the motivation inherent within good work. We'll then expand that into our modern understanding of intrinsic motivation — purpose, mastery and autonomy.

 CHAPTER SUMMARY

Righto, by now you are seeing motivation in a bigger context. There's a gap between where we are and where we want to be — we can call this constructive discontent. In order for a gap to exist, there needs to be a level of aspiration. This can be triggered by inspiration, or by external elements 'activating' a desire for change.

When this aspiration surpasses our internal resistance, we then have a workable motivation gap to play with. The classical approach to motivation is to tackle things internally — to work on attitudes and beliefs. However, this approach is fraught with peril unless you take an incredibly sophisticated approach at an individual level.

The alternative is to default to the classical managerial approaches to motivation — namely, setting goals and rewards. This chapter highlighted the dangers of overemphasising goals, and gave some insight into how you can mitigate some of the dangers associated with rewards.

And now we're left with the third approach — making the work bit work, to bridge the gap between where things are and where we want them to be. It is here we find purpose, mastery and autonomy.

And it is here we find the root of all game-changing hacks.

PART II ▶

GETTING YOUR
GAME ON

4

THE ROOT OF ALL GAME-CHANGING HACKS

The conventional rules miss the fundamental act of good management—managing for progress.

— Teresa Amabile

People ask me what my number one piece of advice is for attaining the motivation to do great work. It's usually at a dinner party or some other social function, and I think they're disappointed by my answer. For three reasons:

1. I get all super-academic-excited.

2. I don't say the usual simple stuff like 'just believe' or 'visualise your success'.

3. The answer is as simple as it is powerful.

Here it is:

Make progress visible.

That's my number one piece of advice. If you stop reading now, and just go out there and reduce the latency between effort and meaningful feedback, then you will have tapped into the most powerful way to amplify and sustain intrinsic motivation.

I sometimes wish there was more magic, mystique and pizzazz to it, something I could sell as some mystical mindset thing. But it's as simple and as complicated as that. Short-circuit feedback loops, and enhance the visibility of progress.

The Progress Principle

It all started with a question: What makes employees enthusiastic about doing work?

Researchers Professor Teresa Amabile and Professor Steven Kramer asked more than 600 managers (from dozens of companies, in different industries, at different levels) to rank five workplace factors commonly considered significant for influencing motivation at work: recognition, incentives and rewards, interpersonal support, a sense of progress, and clear goals.

These are all good answers, of course. But 'recognition for good work' came out on top as the one factor considered by managers as most important for positively influencing motivation.

And it makes sense: if someone does good work and they are applauded in front of the team (or privately), then the work is recognised, which is good. Good work shouldn't just disappear into the void.

(Now, I'm going to take some poetic licence here and just reshuffle the order of Amabile and Kramer's research—it didn't happen quite in the order I describe, but it works for dramatic effect.)

So, the researchers thought, 'Recognition of good work, eh? Hrmm... You know what might be novel? Let's actually ask the employees themselves!' And so they followed a bunch of employees from several different companies over several years, analysing more than 12 000 journal entries to see what correlated to the highest level of motivation at work. It turns out, the thing that was most important was actually what the managers ranked *dead last*.

And the number one thing was—you guessed it—*a clear sense of progress.* Not only was this the number one factor in the research, but this research was also recognised by the *Harvard Business Review* as the number one breakthrough idea in 2010. It's called 'The Progress Principle'.

And this principle makes a whole lot of sense. It's a key feature of games, and *should* be a key feature of all work—robot, ninja or otherwise.

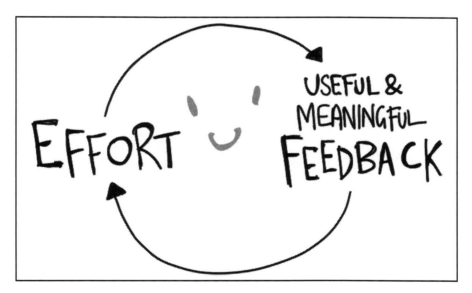

Conservation of effort

You've heard about conservation of energy, right? How energy is neither created nor destroyed; how it only ever changes form, and flows from one place to another? Of course you have. So the total energy of an isolated system always remains the same.

I think a similar approach to motivation is quite useful. Indeed, I'll soon propose that we are 100 per cent motivated all of the time.

But let's get back to the progress principle, because it forms the root of all game-changing hacks. It's the first place you go to if you encounter any kind of challenge to the inherent motivation within an activity.

We have a finite amount of energy and time to invest in things. Oh sure, sometimes we can summon 110 per cent and all that, giving it our all and then some; but this is not a state we can sustain forever. The simple fact is, we get tired, or we run out of time. Or both. We have multiple goals and priorities (and people) competing for our energy and attention. We're only human, and that's awesome because our inherent laziness protects us from overinvesting in activities that won't help us (we've covered this in chapter 1).

Here's what makes a difference: *a clear sense of progress.*

But what does it mean to have a clear sense of progress?

Theoretically, it's when the latency between effort and meaningful feedback is reduced. When we can see how our effort is making a difference and contributing to progress, we are more likely to continue to invest effort into the work. In practice, it looks like:

- an information systems professional finally, after days of searching, finding out why something wasn't working properly
- an executive assistant completing the preliminary draft of an important report
- a sales professional surpassing their personal best
- a factory worker exceeding their daily quota
- a university student completing a practice exam — and so on.

Making progress, moving through constructive discontent — even at the most incremental level — correlates with the highest levels of motivation at work.

And there's a good reason for it: we want to ensure that we invest the finite amount of energy we have each day in something meaningful. Something that is going to contribute to progress towards somewhere or something better. It's one thing to simply work hard at something; it's another to see how that effort correlates to something bigger.

When our sense of progress is low, motivation suffers

Think about this. Imagine you've been given an important research report to work on. It's due Monday, and it's something that will take you most of the week to complete. And you've already got a heap on.

So you work hard, stay back late and even do some extra work on the weekend, cancelling that catch-up with friends for coffee and cupcakes. After a few late nights, you go to submit the report on Monday morning, only to discover that it is no longer needed—the goal has shifted. 'Yeah, we had some meetings with the other executives, and Paul reckons we should tackle a different market', your boss says. Gee, great.

Now, how likely do you think it is that you will replicate the same level of effort for similar work in the future? Not bloody likely, if we're being realistic. Why? Because we're all conservative with our energy—it's not in infinite supply. So perhaps this time you'll put in only the smallest amount of effort, lest the same thing happen again.

And that's what happens when organisations and teams move through change and the process isn't managed well. In situations that do not provide a clear sense of progress, we are uncertain about where best to invest our effort—so we play it safe and invest only what seems to be required.

Our behaviour will default to the activities that provide the richest sense of progress

We just saw what happens when progress is disrupted. Now imagine this: you're working on a project that's both vague and complex. It's not something you or anyone in your team have done before, and you have no idea where to start.

So what do you find yourself doing? Checking emails (and Facebook, and reading unrelated webcomics and articles).

In fact, emails do a great job of giving clear and immediate feedback on progress. You start with 78 emails in your inbox and then, an hour or two later, you've got only 16. Bam—you're winning! Right?

Maybe. But just because our behaviour defaults to activities that provide that richest sense of progress, it doesn't mean that those activities *actually contribute* to any real progress. What we may instead be doing is fuelling the busywork—being efficient, without being *effective.*

I have a friend who procrastibakes. As in she literally bakes a cake as a form of procrastination. Tangible progress! She can stare into the oven and see the cake taking shape. I know people who tidy their desk or clean their house as a form of procrastination, or do meaningless file sorting, or post inane updates on Facebook just to get the feedback of some 'likes'.

All of these activities provide an immediate and visible sense of progress.

So the real challenge or goal is: how do we progress the bigger and more complex stuff that matters? That new strategy, change, progress and growth—all of it incredibly important. And yet we will often default to focusing on small operational wins, rather than progressing the bigger picture.

The solution recalls Kotter's first imperative for change: *a sense of urgency needs to be created.* We need to use the progress principle with game design (oooh) to engineer optimistic urgency for real progress-making work.

A clear sense of progress

You don't need to be making progress in order to get a sense of whether your current approach is working or not. It's the *sense* of progress that matters.

If you are obtaining meaningful information as a result of the effort you invest, then you are more likely to keep investing effort and exploring ways to make progress. The sense of progress sustains autonomy (a key element of intrinsic motivation—the freedom to choose how you go about your work).

This works best if the feedback is given in proximity to the task, with minimal delay. The closer the feedback is in relation to the task at hand, the greater the impact on the sense of progress will be. This is part of the reason why many video games can have players spending 80 per cent of their time failing. The feedback is fast, succinct and relevant to the task at hand.

Most people have a strong intrinsic motivation to do great work—at least early in their careers. And that motivation persists until something gets in the way. The implications of this are very important, and run counter to the conventional rewards-based approach to managing motivation—as long as the work is meaningful, you don't need to cook up fancy ways to motivate your team. 'They are much better served by removing barriers to progress, helping people experience the intrinsic satisfaction that derives from accomplishment', Amabile and Kramer observe.

So if you're managing or leading people, it's your job to keep progress blockers, setbacks and derailment at bay. You'll want to avoid impeding progress by changing goals autocratically (ambushing the team with change), being indecisive or holding up resources without reason.

All of these obstacles are mitigated by a flatter approach to leadership, and when people are kept in the loop about how things are progressing. So setbacks can be anticipated and proactively managed, maintaining forward momentum.

Progress exists in a container

Consider finding one and a half chocolate biscuits in their packet in the fridge. It's like a progress bar, right? And one of the tasks still remains incomplete. It's literally a bite-sized task, so you do your duty. But then there's just one biscuit remaining. It looks a bit silly, sitting there, just one biscuit in a row of empty biscuit slots. There's just one thing left to do — so you eat the biscuit and complete the progress bar. The sense of incompleteness has been resolved. This is winning. And I mean, who leaves one and a half biscuits in a packet anyway?

Any container or vessel is a form of progress bar. It's why you add too much milk to a cup of tea simply to finish off the bottle of milk — the bottle is the progress bar. It's why we work so hard to empty our inbox — it's a container.

When you think about behaviour from this perspective, it becomes ever more important to map out proximal (near-term) milestones to scaffold the journey through meaningful challenge. We'll unpack how games do this in the next chapter, and there's a comprehensive framework we'll unpack in chapter 8.

But at it's simplest level, it's about crafting *containers* to hold progress.

Like a piece of paper with a list of things to do. Writing a list is the simplest type of game you can create for yourself. Many people actually write things they've already completed on their to-do list, just so they can tick them off and get that sense of progress and the satisfaction that comes with it.

There are online tools you can use too. I began writing this book using a website called 750words.com — a simple site that tracks your writing and displays your progress visually. Any day I hit 750 words got a big tick, and that tick didn't disappear — it stayed visible. It has legacy.

750words.com got me back into the habit of writing. Even if I had just spent the whole day in planes in multiple time zones, or had just facilitated a full-day strategy workshop in another country, I'd still (usually) sit down to write 750 words. They may have been crap words, but the game was about *progression*, not perfection.

Other tools may involve a daily checklist on a monthly calendar. If you're looking to build and sustain new habits (like, for example, at least 30 minutes of physical activity each day), then you can simply check those boxes every time you successfully complete the new habit. Eventually you'll have a string of checked boxes appearing on your calendar. Now the new game will be to keep the chain unbroken!

In chapter 8 we'll unpack a model of contextual momentum—something that helps to enhance progress visibility across different levels of time and focus. Look forward to that.

The LinkedIn progress bar

Professional networking site LinkedIn had a significant challenge at one stage—getting people to complete their profiles. Potential new members wanting to get a sense of what LinkedIn was about were greeted with a sea of blank profiles, with no photos and incomplete information. You can imagine it's not the best look. To prospective members assessing whether or not to join, it'd seem like a bit of a ghost town (apart from those self-spruiking social media 'gurus'—you know who I mean). But more importantly, it's critical that sites like LinkedIn establish and support the behavioural norms desired in the community.

Rather than simply default to incentivising people to complete their profiles ('complete your profile and enter for the chance to win one of 500 Amazon gift cards!'), all LinkedIn did was provide a sense of progress for the activity. They added a container for the behaviour—a progress bar for profile completion, ranging from 0 per cent to 100 per cent.

This simple structure tapped into a few things. First, people were getting clear and immediate feedback proximal to the task. If a photo was added to the profile, your profile was an additional 25 per cent complete.

After the core elements were completed, additional, simple tasks were introduced to help progress the bar even further. 'Add your background = +20%' or 'Add in your previous education = +10%'—clear, small, crisp actions. They didn't take long to complete, and again the feedback loops were short.

Finally, as we pass 60 per cent profile completion, our bias to complete tasks within a defined container will kick in, taking most of us to completion. This is just one example of how visibility of progress can be all you need to enhance the inherent motivation of an activity or task. It's the root of all game-changing hacks, the very first thing we need to address if we want to elevate and improve our motivation to do great work.

In fact, sometimes the very concept of 'motivation' can be a distraction to making work work. To tackle this, I have an incorrect theory to propose.

A most incorrect yet utterly useful way to view motivation

I once saw a webcomic of someone lying on the couch doing nothing. The thought bubble read: 'I'm not lazy. I'm 100 per cent motivated to do nothing.'

This struck me as being incredibly profound.

We are all 100 per cent motivated, even when we are not.

Remember how we saw that all beliefs are untrue, but some are useful? Well, it's incredibly flawed for me to say we are 100 per cent motivated all the time (the concept collapses when we look at ways to 'enhance' motivation—for how can one improve upon 100 per cent?)...but it's also an incredibly useful way to view motivation. Stay with me on this.

If everyone is 100 per cent motivated all of the time, then all our actions will be a direct result of our motivation. *What we are doing is what we are motivated to do.* Therefore, given what we know about conservation of effort, and how our behaviour will default to activities that provide the richest sense of progress; if you want to change someone's behaviour, you don't fix the motivation—you fix the work.

In other words, if you want to change behaviour, you *change the game.*

Behaviour change = motivation + ability + trigger

Dr B. J. Fogg, founder of the Persuasive Technology Lab at Stanford University, has developed a rather delightful and very useful behaviour model. You can find out more about B. J. Fogg and his behaviour model at www.behaviormodel.org (he does great work in behaviour design). Using Fogg's eloquent approach to behaviour change, I have expanded his behaviour model into a quadrant (see figure 4.1).

This quadrant covers four domains:

1. the 'too hard' quadrant, where a behaviour is unlikely to occur due to the task being too complex or difficult, and the motivation too low

2. the 'automatic yes' quadrant, where behaviour is likely to occur due to the motivation being high and the task being simple, clear and achievable

3. the 'passion' quadrant, where behaviour change is predominantly reliant upon high motivation.

4. the 'persuasion' quadrant, where behaviour change is predominantly reliant upon the activity being clear, simple and easy to do.

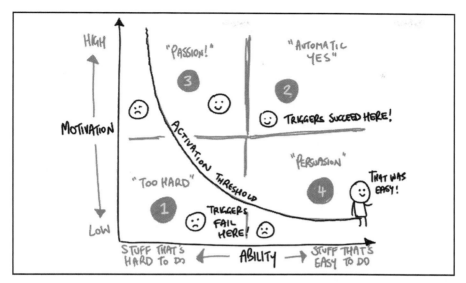

Figure 4.1: the behaviour change quadrant (adapted from the B. J. Fogg behaviour model)

The argument is that for any behaviour to change, three components are needed: motivation, ability and a trigger.

Motivation

Ah now, see here's the thing. If you've been following me so far, you'll see that I've been trying to get a lot of the extraneous junk that clouds and corrupts the inherent motivation of an activity out of the way. And this is a key that B. J. Fogg advocates in his work: you'll get much bigger wins in behaviour change if you just focus on making stuff easier to do.

And besides, we simply cannot maintain high levels of motivation in all things at all times.

Of course, if the task or process is impossible to make easier, and if it lacks any inherently motivating attribute, then the careful and considered use of rewards and other extrinsic motivators is worth exploring.

Ability

There's a lot to be said about self-efficacy—belief in one's ability to achieve a desired or intended outcome. Earlier we discussed suspended disbelief and micro-experiments—how belief can be built through the conducting of experiments and the collection of evidence. Fogg suggests that there are two ways you can go about increasing ability: you can train someone, giving them more skills (that's the hard path); alternatively, you can make the target behaviour easier to do (the better path).

In the next chapter, we're going to talk about instances where you may want to make things more challenging. This may confuse things, but do note: more challenging does not necessarily mean we make things more complex, obscure and difficult.

Simplicity and ability walk hand in hand. In many organisations (even smaller ones), the cognitive burden required to figure out how to progress something—what permissions you have, whose role and responsibility it is, and so on—can all pile up and become too much. And it's here that triggers fail.

One of my clients has executives working in 23 different countries across the Asia–Pacific region. The organisation is going through tremendous organisational change, and I was engaged to see how we might incorporate better motivation strategy and design. Specifically, they wanted to get their executive team working more collaboratively across different functions, and communicating more organically (that is, not simply when mandated or during official meetings).

But oh, the friction! The difficulty in connecting with your counterpart in a different country and progressing meaningful collaboration was a nightmare that simply resulted in more emails clogging up the system. Big developments would happen at central HQ, only for it to be discovered that Japan or Thailand or one of the other countries had gone and taken their own path.

The solution here, as with many things, lay not in simply increasing capability and skill through training, or in trying to increase the motivation to engage in a set of desired behaviours. No, the first thing to focus on was creating an environment where collaborative communication was easier to do.

Triggers

These prompts, cues, requests and calls to action can take a variety forms. It could be an email reminder, a meeting alert, a deadline reminder, an advertisement, a conference, a conversation, the end of a quarter—anything that can facilitate, signal or spark our motivation to engage in a particular activity.

The *activation threshold,* as Fogg describes it, is what determines if a trigger is going to work or not. Behaviour happens when motivation is high, and/or when stuff is simple and easy to do. It's *less* likely to occur when motivation is low, or when stuff is complex and harder to do.

That's why long emails with a heap of open questions like 'Can you tell me what your thoughts are on this?' are less likely to get a response than simple, focused emails like: 'Are you available next Wednesday at 4 pm for a quick (10 min) Skype update about Project X?'

As an aside, TED curator Chris Anderson and TED scribe Jane Wulf once wrote a blog post about the relentless growth of inbox overload. It is driven by a simple fact: 'The average time taken to respond to an email is greater, in aggregate, than the time it took to create.'

The blog post was immensely popular, and has since turned into a global email charter — '10 Rules to Reverse the Email Spiral'. The first rule is key to this book, and relates to motivation and behaviour.

Respect recipients' time.

'This is the fundamental rule', Anderson and Wulf state. 'As the message sender, the onus is on you to minimise the time your email will take to process. Even if it means taking more time at your end before sending.'

You can find out more about The Email Charter at emailcharter.org (a few of my clients have adapted this to shift their organisation's emailing behaviour).

When designing for motivation and behaviour, *the onus is on you to get the game right.*

Here's another example to highlight the activation threshold. And it's a simple one. Imagine you've come across a recipe site. You've bought yourself a Thermomix (a fancy cooking machine that does nearly everything) and you come across a blogger who consistently shares really wonderful recipes. For a long time you bookmark pages or copy and paste from their site, but then after a few months you notice their website has had a facelift. There's also now a little box that says, 'If you like these recipes, please donate to keep this site alive!'. And bam — there's the trigger.

And so, motivated to give the blogger a small donation, you click on the link ... only to be brought to a contact form with multiple fields and a message that says, 'We'll get back to you via email with our banking details'. Gah! Hideous. It even has a CAPTCHA box at the bottom—one of those twisted things that makes you translate some insane scribbles into letters and numbers to prove you're not a computer. In any event, it's all become too hard, you give up and in disgust you burn all the recipes you had collected.

Now, let's take this same scenario—but instead of a contact form, imagine if the blogger simply had a PayPal button that said 'Donate $5'. How easy is that? With one click, you are committed to the path of making the donation. The behaviour occurs through the simplicity and ease of the process.

A lot of this comes down to friction. Once you get visibility around progress and the stuff that matters, the things that stand in the way become ever clearer, and we're better able to do the good work of removing them.

Remove the friction

I get asked a lot to consult on gamification interventions. An abridged conversation usually sounds like this:

Client: Jason! We want to use gamification to make using our CRM [customer relationship management] and sales software more fun!

Me: Why?

Client: Because, err, well people just aren't using it.

Me: Why not?

Client: Ah well, it's pretty clunky. It takes a while to upload information, and there are a lot of fields that need to be completed. And because there are so many fields to complete, most of our team just skips through them, so the data we collect is patchy. So I thought maybe if we add some points, and maybe use badges, leaderboards and other incentives, we can get people to enjoy it more.

Me: Shudder.

Client: Did you just say 'shudder'?

Me: No, I just thought it. But anyway, it sounds to me that we'd be best served by removing the friction in the process first. Let's first get your staff wanting to use the software because it's useful and helps their work, before we get carried away with gamification.

Client: And that's why we pay you the big bucks, my friend! All right, I'll turn off the bat signal. When can you come in?

Okay, honestly I'm not that cool in real-life conversations, and that last part is a lie — but you get the point.

First and foremost, let's make the work work.

Stuff that gets in the way of progress can fall into two categories:

a **Challenges to be solved** — like a puzzle. Creative thinking and possibly collaboration are required, but with the right savvy these roadblocks can be conquered and progress can flow once more.

b **Obstacles beyond staff's immediate control** — like unnecessary protocols and meetings, and extraneous steps and permissions required to progress things. Budget cuts, shifting goals and priorities, and external influences can also put a stop to progress.

In the first instance, the challenge can be good. Provided you haven't contaminated (with extrinsic motivators) the inherent motivation to solve or progress through it, a meaningful challenge is part and parcel of good work.

The second thing is not so good. This friction complicates things and gets in the way. Your role as a leader or manager of people should first be to eliminate and protect your team from as much unnecessary friction as possible.

And it all comes back to visibility of progress and the stuff that matters.

Visibility before accountability

I have several friends who run and go to the gym. If they don't start off with at least 30 minutes of intense physical activity, the rest of their day is buggered up. They feel like something is missing, and they're less productive. It's the 30 minutes that makes all the difference.

Projects, progress and meaningful change need this too — and the effort you make to craft *visibility and structure* around the work that matters is the thing that will make all the difference.

I've worked with organisations struggling through the process of change at a glacial pace. These organisations have a great vision — but the vision has not been captured or communicated in a way that provides a clear sense of progress. There's no container, no clear aspiration, and things are complex. And so people default to conservative efforts and cling to the structures they know.

Having a structure — a list, a Gantt chart, a map or anything that provides some level of contextual visibility of progress — should be the first point of order. And this happens *before* establishing accountability.

Structures — even loose ones cobbled together on the back of a napkin on a week-by-week basis — provide an objective, shared third space. It's in this space that you can be critical and constructive about the work, because it's not directed at an individual, and it's out of the realms of 'fluff' — big words that, on a practical level, mean different things to different people. Without this space to clarify things, and without the ability to talk at a functional, behavioural level, things can derail.

Traits vs behaviours

I sometimes team up with behavioural scientists and psychologists to tackle epic, enterprise-level culture programs. Three of my good mates and fellow conspirators, Darren Hill, Alison Hill and Dr Sean Richardson, are the authors of *Dealing with the Tough Stuff*. Part of their work involves showing leaders and managers how to make the critical distinction between traits and behaviours. 'Your ability to remove the fluff, confusion and assumptions that occur in a conversation comes from stepping out of using trait-based language and gaining clarity through discussing the desired behaviour', they say.

So what are traits?

Traits are words that describe a *collection* of behaviours. Team player, shows initiative, generous, good communicator — all of these are traits. They describe a set of behaviours. So when you say to your team, 'We need to be more proactive and show more initiative', they could translate that into a range of different potential behaviours. And if the conversation is kept at a traits-based level (as it often is), people could be left wondering, does 'be more proactive and show more initiative' mean you want me to:

- start things without seeking approval first?
- do more research, or develop a set of contingency plans for upcoming opportunities and threats?
- work harder and meet milestones even earlier?
- have more personal input into the way the project plays out?

...and so on. As you can see, a conversation at a traits-based level can be fraught with ambiguity. This makes it harder to map out and track the behaviours that contribute to progress.

Better to have the conversation at a behaviour-based level. Behaviours can be observed and measured. They're specific and real.

So, with the right structure in place (the visibility), you can clarify the specific behaviours you want to see more of. To use our 'be more proactive and show more initiative' example, the specific behaviours you might clarify are these:

- We've got deadlines fast approaching, and you have enough experience in this to make the right decisions. I'd like you to feel free to make decisions without seeking my approval first (as long as they aren't for anything over $1000).

- Also, the reporting deadlines we have listed are really the latest possible time they are due—it's more of a deadline for me than for you. I'd like you to submit reports to me at least a day early so I have a chance to read them before submission.

There, now we're talking in behaviour-based language (with a dash of contextual purpose too).

Keeping it real

Hopefully by now you've realised that motivation and organisational change don't have to be mythological and complicated. And they don't require fancy extrinsic motivators or elaborate motivational plots.

Often your biggest wins occur simply by making the 'work' bit work.

Sometimes this means decontaminating the work from well-intended yet counterproductive extrinsic factors, and managing for *progress* rather than motivation.

 **CHAPTER SUMMARY**

In this chapter we've unpacked the simplest and most effective way you can enhance the inherent motivation of any project, process or work—by *making progress visible*. Short-circuit feedback loops, and protect your team from setbacks and delays, or from being ambushed by change. Avoid shifting goals autocratically, and maintain structures that provide context and visibility of the stuff that matters.

A clear sense of progress correlates with the highest levels of motivation at work. We have a limited amount of energy to invest in things, so our behaviour will default to the activities that provide the richest sense of progress.

A clear sense of progress works best when feedback is:

- objective and succinct (that is, not simply an opinion, but data or real evidence one can quickly work with to calibrate further efforts)
- proximal to the behaviour (that is, not delayed by months, but close to the behaviour where it is most relevant and useful)
- frequent (that is, not rare, but readily available when needed).

Progress flourishes within a vessel. By placing a piece of work in a container, you have a defined start point and end point, along with the ability to track relative progress between these two points.

Getting more motivation can work better when we take motivation out of the equation all together. A flawed but incredibly useful way to view motivation is to think of everyone being 100 per cent motivated to act and behave exactly as they do, all the time. Therefore, to change the behaviour, we need to change the game.

To get a desired behaviour, you need to ensure people have the motivation and the ability. Any trigger you have for the behaviour is less likely to work if you don't have both of these factors.

Often, the thing that limits progress and derails behaviour is not a lack of motivation, but rather a deluge of friction between where people are and where we want them to be. By removing the friction and making things easier to achieve, you can achieve big wins in progress and motivation.

Having visibility of progress and the stuff that matters makes it easier for you to engage in behaviour-based conversations. Accountability is easier when people know what game they are playing.

Ultimately, the recurring message is that work can be inherently motivating. Our first approach to enhancing motivation is not to contaminate things with new rewards or schemes, but to amplify the motivation that's already there. Providing a clear sense of progress is the first and most important step.

Crafting the game comes next.

5

GET YOUR HEAD
INTO THE GAME

Reality is broken. Game designers can fix it.

— Jane McGonigal

'Back in my day, we didn't sit around playing video games—we played outside, with a real ball', the stereotypical grandpa passionately reminisces, waving his stick. 'But ah', you think. 'You were still playing games though, right?'

This chapter explores the *game* part of the game changer, taking our newfound savvy in motivation science and combining it with powerful insight from the world of game design.

Is this book part of an elaborate plot to get people to play more video games? Nah, not really. But as I mentioned in the introduction, there's a whole world of savvy in game design that overlaps with good motivation science. And we can use this savvy to do great work.

The myths that surround games

Like the concept of motivation, games also suffer from their own set of myths. So, let's just smash through the three big myths and then get into the anatomy of what makes a game, and how game design can be your best friend if you're trying to progress any meaningful change.

The three big myths are:

Myth #1: 'But games are just for teenage boys, the unemployed and sad divorced men, right?' Ah, so very wrong...

Myth #2: 'People play games because they want to feel like they are winning.' This myth is close to the truth, so let's clarify...

Myth #3: 'People play games to avoid or escape hard work.' Oooh, really? Yeah, we'll smash this one...

Let's look at the truth behind the first myth...

Games are a global phenomenon

In her legendary TED presentation 'Gaming Can Make a Better World', Dr Jane McGonigal shared some of the fascinating research published by Carnegie Mellon University. 'The average young person today in a country with a strong gamer culture will have spent 10 000 hours playing online games by the age of 21', McGonigal says. 'Now 10 000 hours is a really interesting number for two reasons. First of all, for children in the United States 10 080 hours is the exact amount of time you will spend in school from fifth grade to high school graduation if you have perfect attendance.'

Now that's pretty startling. In his very popular book *Outliers*, journalist Malcolm Gladwell popularised the research of Dr Anders Ericsson, who has concluded that 10 000 hours of practice is the key to success and mastery in any particular field.

But while we may have a new generation of master gamers emerging, games are not just for young people. Far from it.

Right now more than 500 million people spend more than 5 *billion* hours each week playing online video games. Most of these are adults. In Australia, the average gamer is 32 years old (compared to an average age of 36 globally). And 43 per cent of people aged over 51 are also gamers, while 47 per cent of gamers are female—in fact, there are more adult female gamers than there are teenage boy gamers.

That's myth #1 busted.

Games are very much an adult thing. And we love playing them—sports games, board games, video games, word games, you name it. Every time I catch a flight, the crosswords, sudoku and other puzzle games in the inflight magazines are *always* already completed. We love playing games.

And when we're not playing games, we're watching them. Sports games and reality TV game shows consistently rank among the most-watched TV shows.

Games, from chess in the west to Go and mahjong in the east, are not unique to any culture. They have been with us since the dawn of civilisation, and *play* has been with us even longer—since before we were *Homo erectus.*

In no way are games just for teenagers of the new generation. As you will soon discover, you've been playing games *your whole life.*

Games are not just about winning

I often ask adults older than me why they think younger folk love games. 'It's because they like winning' is an answer I often get.

To call this one a myth is probably a bit of a stretch, but it *is* a distorted truth. And a sad one too, for if people only play games because they like winning, what does that say about the rest of their life? The extension of this logic is that life is hard, and they simply want to 'escape' responsibility and the tough stuff.

The fact is we love games for the sheer inherent joy they bring—whether we are winning or not. Some studies suggest that video gamers will spend 70 to 90 per cent of their time *failing*. There is joy in the frustration.

Let's look at the classic game of Tetris. You've probably played it before—you have to align falling bricks of various shapes to create a solid row that then activates the bricks in that row to magically disappear. The challenge is that, as the game progresses, you must get faster and faster at deciding how to align the bricks so they disappear before they stack up and hit the top of the screen.

Simple enough, right? Possibly even boring, depending on how you look at it. And yet millions of people have played this game, and continue to play it. (The London Philharmonic Orchestra did a tribute to the game, incidentally.)

But here's the thing: even if you happen to be an absolute ninja champion at Tetris, you will fail. This is a game in which you are *guaranteed* to fail. Everyone who has played Tetris has failed. And everyone who will play Tetris will ultimately fail. And yet people still engage in this game. Why?

Well, it's got something to do with the inherent sense of progress, and the mastery that comes from benchmarking your score. But it's also got a lot to do with *flow*—the art of optimal experience.

Mihaly Csikszentmihalyi (pronounced *CHEEK-sent-me-HIGH-ee*—easy, right?), a professor of psychology at Claremont Graduate University, has dedicated his life to exploring the psychology of optimal experience.

In 1975 Csikszentmihalyi published a breakthrough scientific study called *Beyond Boredom and Anxiety*. He found that, by engaging in challenging endeavours with a clear purpose, well-established rules for action, clear feedback and the potential for increased difficulty, one could achieve deep, effortless involvement. This is where you are so engaged with the task that worries slip away, and 'concern for the self disappears, yet sense of self emerges stronger'.

Csikszentmihalyi wrote that 'games are an obvious source of flow', and argued that the failure of schools, offices and workplaces to provide for flow was one of the most serious and urgent moral issues facing humanity. 'If we continue to ignore what makes us happy, we … perpetuate the dehumanising forces which are gaining momentum day by day', he wrote.

Games aren't just about winning; they are about developing mastery and progressing through meaningful challenge. This is something many people miss when attempting to 'gamify' work—they focus on 'reward' elements and make winning too easy. But rewards without meaningful challenge are *meaningless*.

The challenge comes first. In fact, it could be argued that most games are simply well-designed, challenging work.

Games are simply work that's well designed

The myth is that people play games because they want to avoid challenging work. The reality is, people play games to engage in *well-designed*, challenging work. The only thing they are avoiding is poorly designed work. In essence, we are replacing poorly designed work with work that provides a more meaningful challenge and offers a richer sense of progress.

And we should note at this point that just because something is a game, it doesn't mean it's good. As we'll soon see, it can be argued that *everything* is a game. The difference is in the *design*.

Really good games have been ruthlessly play-tested and calibrated to the point where achieving a state of flow is almost guaranteed for many. Play-testing is just another word for iterative development, which is essentially the conducting of progressive experiments. In other words: science.

Let's look at the game of golf. I'm not a golfer (as a red-headed descendant of Vikings, the sun is my arch-nemesis), but here's an interpretation.

So the goal of golf is to get the ball in the hole with the least number of shots. If I was a productivity expert, I'd be advocating for spending the least amount of time on the golf course. After all, if you want to achieve your objective of getting the ball into the hole with the least number of shots, you could simply drive right up to the hole, get out of the golf cart, line up your shot and sink the ball in the hole in one shot, thereby minimising your exposure to the sun and the time spent in the pursuit or execution of your goal—winning.

Now, if I was an efficiency expert who was helping you leverage things better, I could talk about how the game of golf could be improved by replicating the ball and hole at a location more proximal to you—like having a hole drilled in your desk at work. This way, you can drop balls into it, and thereby win, at any point in the day. Even better, if I was a systems expert, I could suggest that we set up a tubular device so you could have balls running through this hole 24/7, thereby providing a *constant* state of winning, even in your sleep. And yet, games don't work like this. They have *rules* to make them challenging.

Games work *because* they are challenging. People play games because the challenges are well-designed work.

Play theorist Brian Sutton-Smith says, 'The opposite of play is not work—it's depression'.

In fact, people will *pay money* to do well-designed work. *World of Warcraft,* that game I used to be an alchemist for, costs money to play each month. At its peak it had more than 12 million registered users paying US$15 a month to spend an average of 80 hours each month inside the game. That's the equivalent of holding down a part-time job.

But games don't have to be flashy, with multi-million dollar budgets invested in design and development. Even with simple game structures, people have united to do real work to tackle real-world issues.

For example, researchers created a puzzle game called Foldit, which was designed to simulate actual protein folding. It's kind of like a Rubik's Cube, except flexible, more complex and not a cube at all. The idea was that human players could come up with more interesting solutions to real-life problems than the artificial intelligence that scientists were relying on could.

This hypothesis was recently confirmed when scientists decided to put a particularly tricky puzzle in the game—a puzzle with an answer that had been eluding researchers for a decade. Ten days later it was solved, leading to a major breakthrough in AIDS research.

So good games are well-designed work. Game design can be conceived along very similar lines to project design, process design, work design and ... *progress* design. In fact, there are massive overlaps.

There's just one problem. The word 'game'.

The trouble with the word 'game'

Some of us distrust the word 'game'. It took me a while to realise this, as early on in my consulting practice we used game design and words like 'gamefulness' quite heavily. But while some love it, it does make many people a bit uncomfortable.

I have three theories as to why. The first two are minor—the third is major.

Theory the first: we are supposed to 'work hard'. Many people's parents grew up during war and recessions, when things were tough. The thought that work could be playful is too close to the thought that work could be pleasurable. And pleasure is a sin. We must suffer, and therefore avoid things that sound like fun.

Theory the second: work is serious. Many of us work in organisations that are incredibly risk-averse. To the point that the organisational immune system that protects it from radical ideas actually starts to attack itself, hobbling innovation and progress. If someone says, 'Come on guys, this isn't a game', they are indicating that things need to be taken seriously.

The wonderful philosopher James Carse had some thoughts on seriousness. He writes that 'to be serious is to press for a specified conclusion; to be playful is to allow for possibility whatever the cost to oneself'. And so we have environments of blandness, where the same suits all pile in, push their agendas and use the same lifeless corporate speak to crush daring authenticity whenever it is encountered, leaving no room for games and play.

Theory the third: no one likes a 'playa'. If someone in a nightclub described themselves to you as a 'playa', someone who knows how to 'play the game', you'd probably be a bit disturbed by them. Indeed, there is a very popular book called *The Game* that shows men how to take a very sophisticated (and manipulative) approach to seduction and 'picking up'.

Someone who says 'Don't play games with me' essentially means 'Don't try to manipulate me'.

But here's the thing: that's what games do.

Games are behavioural manipulation

Games are the parameters designed to influence human motivation and behaviour.

And here's the other thing: it's inescapable. *Everything is manipulation.*

Several studies have shown that background music in a store influences how people spend and buy, plate size influences our perception of taste, and the wording of an email headline will enhance or diminish the likelihood that you will open it. The clothes you wear influence how people perceive you. The tone of your voice influences how people hear you. And so on. At every level, in every way, we are engaged in games and processes that manipulate.

It's just that most of the games we play—the games that matter—are poorly designed, or barely designed at all. In many ways we are not yet tapping into the incredible ability we have to tweak and craft the parameters that influence motivation and behaviour. Or we're doing so in an incredibly clumsy way.

Earlier, I touted the saying 'The house always wins'. It's one of my favourite lines, because it's so true. And worth repeating—because *games always favour their maker.* If you're not playing a part in designing the game you are playing, you are probably being played.

The good news is: we can lift our game, get our head into the game and change the game. But to do that, we need to understand the anatomy of what makes a good game.

THE [TOM] SAWYER EFFECT

It's nigh on impossible to talk about game design and work at any deep level without mentioning Mark Twain's classic tale, written in 1876, *The Adventures of Tom Sawyer.* If you're familiar with it, do move on; if not, come hither, because this is important.

This story is delightfully obscure, however. Take this quote, for example, and you'll see what I mean:

> Jim shook his head and said: 'Can't, Mars Tom. Ole missis, she tole me I got to go an' git dis water an' not stop foolin' roun' wid anybody. She say she spec' Mars Tom gwine to ax me to whitewash, an' so she tole me go 'long an' 'tend to my own business—she 'lowed she'd "tend to de whitewashin".'

So, let me paraphrase a key component of the story. Aunt Polly sends Tom out to whitewash the fence. A friend passes by, and Tom tries to get him to do some of the whitewashing in return for a special kind of marble. He almost agrees, but then Aunt Polly appears and chases him off, leaving Tom alone with his labour.

A little while later another boy Tom's age walks by. Tom convinces him that whitewashing a fence is a great joy. After some bargaining, Ben agrees to give Tom his apple in exchange for the privilege of working on the fence. Over the course of the day, every boy who passes ends up staying to whitewash, and each one gives Tom something in exchange. By the time the fence has three coats, Tom has collected a hoard of miscellaneous treasures. 'Tom had discovered a great law of human action, without knowing it', Twain writes. 'In order to make a man or a boy covet a thing, it is only necessary to make the thing difficult to attain.'

And this is what Daniel Pink and others refer to as the 'Sawyer Effect' — the ability to turn work into play by focusing on the mastering of a challenge.

But there are two sides to the Sawyer Effect. On one side, work can be turned into play, where people will *pay* for the opportunity. The shadow side is where play turns into work (and not in a good way). This often occurs when incentives and rewards are introduced into a system.

How does this happen? We've covered some of the dangers of extrinsic motivators in earlier chapters, but here's a new element: by adding an extrinsic, contingent reward to something, you do three things:

- You communicate that you believe the task to be inherently unmotivating (hence the need to incentivise).

- You contaminate or displace whatever inherent motivation is in the activity.

- You reduce the element of mastery — it becomes much more about doing what is required to obtain the reward, rather than about contributing to longer-term mastery and growth.

The lesson? Be careful with how you introduce motivation design, especially if you are using extrinsic elements. Just as work can become play, play can become work.

The anatomy of a game

Games are simply the interplay of goals, rules and feedback. A good game is a goal-driven, challenge-intense and feedback-rich experience geared towards making progress.

All games — whether they are puzzles, sports games, strategy games, roleplaying games, simulation games, training games or video games — share the same essential three ingredients: goals, rules and feedback (see figure 5.1, overleaf).

Figure 5.1: the three core elements of all games

But here's the thing: nearly every other element of life shares those same three components. So nearly everything in life is a game.

Any project is a game. There are goals (complete this project to bring the prototype into the next phase of implementation), rules (do it in less than six weeks, and with less than $30 000), and feedback.

Each of these elements has the potential to be tweaked up into something better, and to work in better cohesion with the other elements.

So let's have a look at each in more detail.

Goals

Every game has a goal or purpose to it. It may be as simple as solving a puzzle, overcoming a small challenge or completing a task. And it may be epic, like curing cancer or getting the world to adopt cleaner energy.

I gave goals a bit of a hard time in chapter 3. This is mainly due to my experience of goal setting being treated as a default, over-the-counter panacea to any motivational challenge. I used to teach SMART goal setting, and I used to get a lot of work doing this in schools. It was an easy box for teachers to tick, and part of the default motivational folklore. You hit final year, you need goals.

And yet very few of the teachers I spoke with actually had or used SMART goals. In the teacher professional development I ran with many schools and universities, many struggled to gain clarity on their own goals, and very few (if any) had actually captured them in a SMART goal format. The same can also be said of principals. And of most people. SMART goals work if you are setting them yourself (if it floats your boat), and if you are creating structure around routine/robot work, but they fail dismally at aspirational, progress-making ninja work.

Does this mean we abandon goals? Heck no. They are still a very important element in the process (alongside rules and feedback).

We just desperately need to broaden our understanding of how goals work. Because they are an essential ingredient of any good game (and the aspirational element that fuels constructive discontent itself).

There are five types of goals we can use. Each of these occurs at a different level of context—from big picture, purpose-based goals right through to crisp, detailed, task-based goals.

Purpose-based goals

These are your big fuzzy goals. They are the overarching vision, and the most epic of all goal types.

Many roleplaying games will periodically provide you with a world-level context, showing how your actions contribute to big, purposed-based goals—saving the world, conquering the evil overlord and so on. In *World of Warcraft*, you literally start with a panning, narrative tour across the whole world.

But in real-world work we sometimes lose that perspective, and instead only see the immediate tasks that need to be done. This can erode the sense of purpose we feel in our work, which is unfortunate, as we are often happiest when we are contributing to something bigger than ourselves (and most motivated when we can see how our efforts contribute to a clear sense of progress towards a bigger vision).

Too many leaders don't aim high enough, and keep their goals limited to measurable objectives. In chapter 2 we had a look at some vision statements, including Apple's manifesto 'Think Different'. We also reviewed Professor Kotter's thoughts on why transformational change fails—not having (or communicating) a clear vision is one of the most critical factors.

Purpose-based goals are generally:

- very big picture
- qualitative (that is, words not numbers)
- epic, inspiring and a little audacious
- not terribly specific
- hard to measure.

But beneath the umbrella of big, far-reaching visions, we have quest-based goals.

Quest-based goals

Quests are nested within a bigger purpose — in other words, completing a quest contributes to a higher-level goal.

Quests are usually the following:

- **Narrative and change-driven.** Questing is what is usually done when you are attempting to explore a new solution, and progress is measured more in the sense of emerging clarity than in specific numbers. It's how the story progresses.
- **Journey-focused.** The outcome is usually not known, and the pathway to achieving it has no clear precedence (for example, 'find a better way to onboard customers').
- **Moderately hard to measure.** You need good structures and rituals to measure the progress of quests, as they are often fraught with tangled pathways, rich failure and learning.

It's not coincidence that the word 'question' begins with a quest. The reverse is also often true: every quest begins with a question — usually along the lines of 'How can we do X better?'

Quests nest the missions that contribute to answering this question.

Mission-based goals

Here we have a quantifiable goal, often with a fairly specific pathway. Unlike a quest (which begins with a clear premise), you are moving towards a clear *promise*.

Missions can be reverse-engineered. They can be broken down into sequenced groups of tasks. They're easy to measure, and the outcome of a mission is usually dualistic — mission success, or mission not-yet-success. In other words, success is easy to measure — it's clear and tickable.

A mission is essentially a project. It's at this point we start to have clear, tangible outcomes.

I love the project mindset. It's focused on achieving (or shipping) a clear outcome, not merely persisting with goals and noble intent. Mission-based goals begin to weave in the rules that make stuff real (more on that soon).

But... I have come to learn that not everyone appreciates projects in the same way. People sometimes don't experience the same optimistic urgency I've felt when embarking on an important project. This is usually because most projects within organisations have been bogged down by a top-down waterfall approach, hobbled by a ridiculous level of planning. The planning gets in the way of the doing, and while I love visibility of progress, it's one thing to have an overarching contextual Gantt chart, and quite another to have a detail-laden beast hidden away in clunky software, where most effort is spent updating it rather than doing the work.

That's why I sometimes use the word *mission*. When you say 'I'm on a mission', it carries a level of *conviction* with it.

I'll even go so far as to work up mission code-names with some of my clients. 'Operation Clevermake' and 'Operation Datashine' are a couple of examples of code-names we've used.

A good mission will use all of the elements of goals and game design. Here's an example of how a well-crafted mission can begin. Imagine you're an executive leader of a mattress and bedding company, and you are facilitating a meeting with your managing directors.

> Righto team, as you know, we're all on a quest to be the best manufacturer and service provider in our industry by reputation [quest]. Part of that involves getting five-star accreditation in sustainability across all of our functions [mission]. And it's a good thing to do—because we're all about changing the world by making people happier through better sleep, and they'll rest easier knowing we're a sustainable company [purpose]. And besides, it's what we should be striving for anyway. So, here's what we need to do: each department, from manufacturing to sales to admin, has a checklist of requirements we need to surpass.* Specifically, we all need to do a gap analysis to see where we already surpass accreditation standards and where we fall short [task]. Let's aim to get this done before our teleconference next week. Just upload your checklists to Basecamp when they are done, so we can see the overlaps.**

> * Refers to broad contextual progress map, which we discuss in chapter 8.
> ** Basecamp is a collaborative, cloud-based project management tool, and here we are seeing a clear parameter for the first set of tasks for the mission.

Just as quest-based goals are made up of mission-based objectives, these in turn are made up of specific tasks.

Task-based goals

Ah, and here is where you can be as SMART as you like. But, while you can technically call them goals, at this level it's more appropriate to call task-based goals 'actions' or 'action steps'.

Just as a journey of a thousand miles begins with a single step, any meaningful progress in missions and quests begins with a single action. Followed by many, many more.

These are the little things that contribute to progress. We want these to be specific, measurable, achievable, realistic and time-based. We want them to be 'crisp' and tickable.

A note on automated goals

You've got a set of core survival drivers that you don't need to think about too much — when you're hungry, you'll have a goal to eat. You've also got established routines — the automation of tasks into systems and patterns of behaviour designed to reduce cognitive burden and enhance efficiency. These are good when all is working. It's when things are not, or when we want to change, that we need to disrupt the pattern with a new game.

As soon as you have a goal, you have a game.

If you've worked on an assignment, submitted a report, gone for a jog, cooked a meal, read a book, climbed a tree — or almost anything else — you've played a game. As soon as there's a goal, there's a game.

It's just that often the goal isn't clear. There's no purpose, no narrative or meaning. Or the goal is *too* clear — it has collapsed to a level of concreteness that denies space for necessary creativity and autonomy. Or there are conflicting goals or shifting targets that encourage conservation of effort. Or the goals are too remote and appear unreachable.

Or ... the goal is fine, but the issue lies in the other elements of the game — the rules and the way you get feedback.

Rules

'Do not pass go. Do not collect $200.'

— Monopoly

Rules get a bad rap. And it's no wonder, because many organisations are clogged up with redundant rules that impede progress. Relics that may have served a purpose in another time, but now time's changed and they're getting in the way. 'Rule breakers' are the true leaders, visionaries and mavericks. So if we want to aspire to be like them, we need to break the rules, right?

No. We have an overly romantic notion about breaking rules, but the reality is we need to *make* them just as much as we need to break them. Rules, when used well, can work tremendously to enhance focus, empower action and facilitate progress. Here are a few of the key benefits.

Rules can be used to calibrate the level of challenge. Too much challenge, and people get anxious or avoid the work. Too little, and people become bored and disengaged, or do not prioritise it. Just right—and we have the chance of getting things into flow.

Some organisations (particularly software developers) run 'hack days' or 48-hour 'hackathons' to create a sense of urgency around the important innovation work no one usually has time for. The normal rules and structure of work are suspended for a finite period of time in exchange for new rules that ramp up the challenge dramatically. This takes place in an environment designed to enhance creativity, productivity and collaboration. For example, we have set up ping-pong tables and provided teams with barista-made coffee during the 48-hour event (more on this soon).

Rules reduce uncertainty *…* by making you more certain about constraints. Every project or process has its constraints—budgets, timelines, suppliers, important clients, key stakeholders, and so on. And every game has constraints—rules that govern when and how you can act.

Take chess, for example. The king moves only one square, the rook can only move in a straight line, and the bishop can only move in a diagonal. One might find such rules confining, and yet they are what underpin the deep strategy in games of chess. New stratagems in this ancient game are still being constructed today.

By proactively seeking constraints early, you are better able to develop and explore emergent strategies (rather than being surprised by setbacks along the way).

Rules are what make up a game. They influence the motivational dynamics at play. For example, you can have a set of rules that will encourage and support more competition, drive and performance among individuals. With a few tweaks you can shift the motivational dynamics (and therefore the behaviour, and eventually the culture) to something much more collaborative.

Back when I lectured at three different universities, I'd see this all the time. In some of the units I developed and coordinated I was able to set the rules and tailor the assessments. So for units such as Environmental Education we'd have a combination of individual projects culminating in a bigger project and internal conference about how they went about making a difference. The rules got students working with each other, and with other researchers globally.

But some of the units I taught were inherited from other lecturers — and often these would contain simple research essays and assignments to be completed with an exam at the end of semester. In the worst case, one university had rules akin to a bell-curve for grading essays and papers. This would mean that, no matter how hard I tried to give everyone attention and support, and provide the best learning opportunities, only 20 per cent of the class could achieve a High Distinction (a mark above 80 per cent). This sucked, and was part of the reason I left the realms of academia. But the rules also created an unhealthy competitive dynamic among the students.

Whereas in other universities and units students were able to support each other freely, in this particular university it was in their interest to *not* help each other. Because doing so might just bump you outside of the 20 per cent that could attain the highest mark. So the learning and motivational dynamics suffered as a result of the rules. There was less sharing between students — other than little 'cliques' that would evolve. There were fewer questions within the lecture, but many more students would approach me individually *after* the lecture (potentially so the whole class might not benefit from any deeper insight that would occur if a question was asked in front of the class). It was annoying and counterproductive. But I should emphasise that a good proportion of students were on international scholarships: they *had* to perform well or their funding would get cut.

Rules shape experience, and we'll be discussing this more in chapter 8.

Ultimately, with all of this talk of 'rule breaking', it's important to remember that we also have the ability to *make* rules. Rules that govern and influence our own behaviour, and rules that shape the motivational dynamics within teams.

Feedback

Feedback is all about progress, and how clear your sense of it is. In most conventional games, feedback on progress is clear and immediate. In other games ... not so much. Feedback gets delayed. But there are some ways we can reduce the latency — including by meeting more frequently but for a shorter duration. Or by using tools, such as collaborative online Gantt charts or real-world progress walls that help to make progress more visible. Feedback is quantitative or qualitative.

Quantitative feedback is essentially numerical. It's the raw data you receive. It's cold and it does not lie, nor does it care what you think or feel about it. I sometimes wish for soft qualitative feedback when I hop onto the scales (especially after writing a long book!), but quantitative data ultimately provides the purest information. It's clear, objective and uncontaminated by intention and meaning (except, of course, the meaning, bias and distortion you bring to it).

One way I've used quantitative feedback is to enhance my fitness. Combining an electronic scale that sent my lean body-mass percentage to an online app paired up with an iPhone app called RunKeeper enabled me to see progress in my health and fitness — something that was incredibly hard to visualise before.

I could see how far, how fast and how frequently I was running. And I could also see how that correlated over time to better lean body-mass. This type of progress is incredibly motivating.

You need to be careful what measures are used to generate quantitative feedback. Because collapsing complexity into a single number will narrow focus, quantitative measures better suited to proximal/shorter-term activities (things that can easily be broken down into clear components) rather than distal/longer-term goals.

In other words, you could use quantitative feedback to measure the *number* of discrete ideas generated in a workshop (if quantity was your game). But it would be inappropriate to measure the *quality* of ideas in the same workshop using a quantitative measure (like a score out of 10).

You can use quantitative feedback in a number of ways but, as always, the first thing to look at is how you can use it to provide a clear sense of progress *during* the activity. Dial up the inherent motivation of the process, rather than anchoring feedback to the end result.

This could be seen as tapping into the Hawthorne Effect — a research bias anyone dealing with human behaviour needs to be aware of. The Hawthorne Effect was originally discovered when researchers conducted experiments on the effect of lighting on productivity in factories in the mid 1920s. It was discovered that *both* the test group (those exposed to modified lighting) and the control group (those working under the usual lighting conditions) increased productivity and performance. The reason? The control group was aware that its productivity and performance were being observed.

It's a good thing to keep in mind if you're conducting experiments involving human behaviour — people's performance may naturally increase due to the very fact they are being observed.

But games take this to a new level. With games, you *know* you're being observed. You're committed to playing the game, not just watching from the sidelines.

Even if you're playing a game solo, you can use the Hawthorne Effect to your benefit. We see this with food diaries. Tracking and recording what you have eaten each day raises your consciousness of your desired behaviour. What's even better is to take photos of your meals *before* you eat them. That way the effect is much more apparent and immediate. Better still if your photos automatically upload into a dropbox shared with an accountabilibuddy. Now we've got a real game happening!

Qualitative feedback includes the non-numerical information you receive about progress. I sometimes like to refer to this as the emerging narrative that accompanies progress. If you were to imagine your work, project or life as a story, qualitative feedback would make up the chapters. When you are able to *reflect* on milestones achieved, qualitative feedback can consolidate and amplify the sense of progress felt by the team. I call this the 'look how far we've come' version of qualitative feedback.

When you assess milestones not achieved, qualitative feedback can reframe potentially demoralising failures into something more constructive. I call this the 'look at what we've learned' version of qualitative feedback.

And when you are able to *project* (as in, forecast) the milestones yet to be achieved, qualitative feedback can lift anticipation for the work ahead. I call this the 'call to adventure' version of qualitative feedback.

But all of these are forms of feedback we receive from someone interpreting the situation through their own filter and biases, so the feedback is not quite as pure as the feedback provided by quantitative data. You need to take it with a pinch of salt, and make your own assessment too (which, of course, will also be flawed with your own bias).

The best approach to feedback is a blended one.

Airbnb—an online platform that connects homeowners with a spare room or a vacant apartment with travellers wanting to rent a place to stay—uses a combination of qualitative and quantitative data to provide a more accurate reflection of customer experience. Many sites do the same. The quantitative data provides comparability (number of stars, percentage that would recommend, and so on) and the qualitative data provides context (what was it *really* like?).

I mentioned how I used RunKeeper for quantitative feedback on fitness progress (how fast, far and frequently I ran). Well here's a nifty thing you can add to nearly *anything* to make it work better: zombies.

I mentioned this earlier—in combination with apps to track your running performance, you can also download and use an app like *Zombies, Run!*

It adds a qualitative *narrative* layer over the game of running. When I don my running clothes and embark on a run, my iPod loops me into a world in which I am one of the few survivors of the zombie apocalypse. As a runner, I am tasked with several important missions: running to the hospital to find first aid kits, going to the old fuel depot to get supplies, or scouting out a new area. My activities are monitored by a chap in a helicopter, who is able to communicate with me via radio link. It's all wonderfully voiced by good British actors. The suspended disbelief kicks in — it actually *feels* real!

So when the helicopter guy looking out for me tells me that zombies are approaching my position — I run! An alert from the app starts in my head: 'Zombies approaching, 60 metres'. The zombies get closer and closer: 'Oh crap — 40 metres'. I can hear them now, groaning as they lope towards me: 'Gah! 20 metres'. If I don't pick up my pace I might lose some of the precious supplies I've collected for the township of survivors. So I run, pushing myself even harder. Anyone else would just see some red-headed chap with white thighs and wild eyes running like his life depended on it.

And hew … does this work! I run faster and further when playing this game.

Use quantitative feedback for shared milestones and targets, and for self-set goals over short distances for focused tasks.

Use qualitative feedback to contextualise quantitative feedback — during key milestone events to amplify the sense of progress, and during potential setbacks to enhance broader thinking.

Goals, rules, feedback — the ultimate diagnostic

If there is anything wrong with a project or process, it usually comes down to goals, rules or feedback. These are what make up the games we play. Either the purpose isn't compelling or relevant, or the goals are too vague (or too tight). Or the rules are obstructive, or the constraints aren't known, or they shape dynamics incongruent to the purpose. Or the feedback latency is too high, or the quality and usefulness of feedback is low.

People love and play games not simply because they are games—life is full of games, and most of them are terribly designed. The best games, however, have been rigorously play-tested. We may not have the luxury of multi-million dollar budgets to do this (as many blockbuster video games have), but we can take a similar, agile and experimental approach.

The elements of games—goals, rules, feedback—provide the ultimate diagnostic to assess any motivation, progress or behaviour-change challenge. All issues lie within these three filters.

And here's a parallel lens for you.

Challenge, stimulation, reward — the three keys to unlocking engagement

My mother always told me there are at least three sides to every story. So I want to propose at least three ways to look at any motivation or progress challenge.

We've already covered a lot of ground with goals, rules and feedback. Now let's look at challenge, stimulation and reward (see figure 5.2).

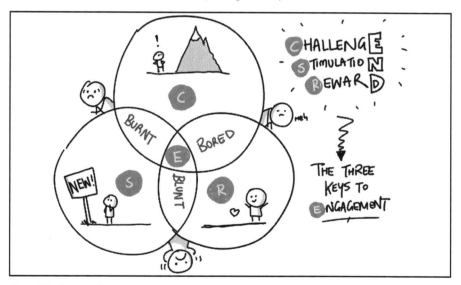

Figure 5.2: the three keys to engagement

I sometimes think of the three elements of challenge, stimulation and reward as spotlights on a stage. All three lights need to be centred on the subject—if one spotlight is out, then we get a shadow. If we want to avoid people getting bored, blunt or burned, we need to get all three elements right.

Challenge

This is critical in the work we do (within organisations, and within our own life). We didn't evolve to be constantly content. Challenge is the companion to all change, progress and growth. Without challenge, we don't collect experience points, and we don't 'level-up'.

If you're leading change, or in charge of work or a project that matters, you need to be able to help calibrate the level of challenge to keep people in flow.

Stimulation

People aren't robots, as much as their work may be robotic. And while some work will inevitably be formulaic, with a heap of repetition, we need to keep work fresh by disrupting patterns, staying open to new pathways, and allowing for freedom and autonomy in how people approach work.

Even with incredibly routine work, stimulation can be found by simply asking people to find or think up better ways to do things. Let them take some ownership over the innovation and improvement-making in their work.

Disrupt patterns of behaviour where appropriate, to prevent people settling into complacency. Explore what-if scenarios, and ask the question, 'If we were to start again today, what would we do differently?'

Reward

By now you know I don't just mean extrinsic rewards. The work itself must connect to something inherently rewarding and meaningful for people. This is usually achieved when people can see how their effort contributes to something bigger than themselves. And it's even better if that something bigger is aligned with their internal values.

But of course, sometimes we need to use extrinsic rewards cautiously—as a light seasoning to what is otherwise good work. The savvy you've accumulated so far should protect you from the major pitfalls associated with extrinsic rewards.

Avoid getting blunt, bored or burned

If you've been to a live theatre performance, you'll have noticed that key characters are usually illuminated by three spotlights. With just two spotlights, you'll get a shadow on stage.

It's much the same with challenge, stimulation and reward. Miss one element, and there'll be a shadow effect.

If there's no challenge, your skills won't be used and you won't stay sharp —you'll get blunt. Many people leave their jobs in pursuit of a greater challenge.

If there's no stimulation, you'll get bored. Boredom is the worst type of apathy. It's the erosion of curiosity and occurs when avenues for exploration have been cut off or denied.

If there's no reward, you'll get burned. Many people work hard through different challenging work—but reach a point where they've forgotten why they're doing it. In essence, they burn out, and usually need some time out to rediscover purpose and meaning in their work.

You can avoid having your people get blunt, bored or burned by keeping these game design lenses in mind at all times.

Furthermore, we need to keep the END in mind too—literally crafting end-points and breaking work down into milestones so that we can see progress.

And now for the third lens (three sides to every story)...

The uncanny parallels

The third lens has actually been covered. Daniel Pink unpacks it in his book *Drive: The Surprising Truth About What Motivates Us.* Pink identifies three overarching elements of intrinsic motivation—purpose, mastery and autonomy. All of these elements align with good game design, as shown in figure 5.3 (overleaf).

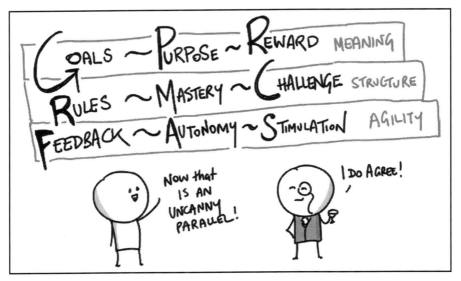

Figure 5.3: the overlap between motivation science and game design

The three core elements of game design (goals, rules, feedback) can be seen as the *structure* that brings to life our modern insight into motivation (purpose, mastery and autonomy).

Goals align with purpose, and the inherent reward of the work.

Rules calibrate challenge, which contributes to mastery.

Feedback enhances the stimulation that keeps people working with autonomy.

 CHAPTER SUMMARY

Earlier I mentioned how, after reading this book, you'll never be able to view work, change and any motivational challenge the same way again. We are nearly at that point.

Games, like motivation, carry their own share of stigma. But when we look at the commonalities between all games—sports games, board games, video games, simulation games, roleplaying games, strategy games and so on—they all share the same underpinning ingredients: goals, rules and feedback.

The reason games work is not because they are games; it's because the goals, rules and feedback—the *elements* of all games and work—are well designed. A good game is a goal-driven, challenge-intense and feedback-rich experience, geared towards progress.

There are many ways to express goals—from big, fuzzy, qualitative and contextual, purpose-based goals; to specific, crisp, measurable, quantitative task-based goals. Finding the right combination of goal elements is key to getting the game right.

Games also don't exist without rules. Games work whenever there is agreement—they collapse whenever there is uncertainty as to how the rules work. Rules provide the scaffolding that allows people to act with clarity and confidence within any given context. Sometimes rules need to be updated to maintain relevance within an evolving context. Rules shape experience and influence the motivational dynamics at play.

And feedback—the root of all game-changing hacks. Games thrive on feedback, and the best feedback provides useful quantitative and qualitative information, proximal to the activity.

Goals, rules and feedback correlate with our modern understanding of intrinsic motivation: purpose, mastery and autonomy.

There's always a game at play.

It's not about turning work into a game—it's about recognising that work *already is* a game. It has goals, rules and feedback. Sometimes we just need to change the game, to make it work better.

So far, we've explored only the *finite* games that occur within life and work. There's at least one other type of game, which we'll unpack in the next chapter, along with the overarching 'game changer' model that will change your life.

A MODEL
GAME CHANGER

Only that which can change can continue: this is the principle
by which infinite players live.

— James Carse

This book could have started with this chapter. I toyed with the notion, but found I had to do so much backtracking that I flipped it again. After all, even with the best intentions it's dangerous to start playing with motivational dynamics unless you have the right focus and approach.

And so here we are! By now you are ready to start exploring how we go about finding the game-changing element. *Games* of course being the interplay of goals, rules and feedback; and the *game changer* being that newly introduced element that creates a significant difference to the existing game.

How do we find the game changer? By combining our understanding of what really motivates people to do great work (purpose, mastery and autonomy), and using the right mix of challenge, stimulation and reward to get the game right. And how do we achieve the right mix? By conducting *experiments*, like an agile ninja scientist.

So that brings us to where we are now. But *making clever happen* is not just about using the science — we also need to bring the philosophy and art of games into the equation.

A theory of fun

'Let's make work fun!' ... are four words that often make me frown. The intention is good, but often people approach the concept of fun from a very superficial level. Like introducing a fickle competition and rewards, or creating distracting rules that interrupt the flow of work. And then things get tacky and lame, very quickly.

A better approach is to first say, 'Let's make work *work!*' ... because fun (and satisfaction) will *follow* good work. In other words, get the game right first. Think *functional* before fun.

But, assuming we've dealt with unnecessary friction, have tightened feedback loops, calibrated challenge and are working towards an appropriate goal — *then* we can start to make things fun. There are a few theories about fun.

Raph Koster, author of *A Theory of Fun for Game Design*, says that fun is just another word for learning. We get the most fun, and therefore the most learning, when we play in optimal conditions (the state of *flow* we discussed in chapter 5, where you are challenged beyond your comfort zone — but not too much so). Many young mammals play as a way of learning, and it could be argued that the experience of fun is a natural reward for learning important survival skills.

Yet people can experience fun even when they are not necessarily learning anything, so other theories divide fun into different categories—like *soft fun* and *hard fun*.

Phallic connotations aside, soft fun is a term that's used to describe passive activities—like going to the movies, watching TV, seeing a comedy show. 'That was fun', someone says, and people mumble their agreement.

Hard fun is a term that could be used to describe challenging but well-designed, progress-making work. Like, oh I don't know, working with the team all weekend to prototype a new product, working with friends to renovate a house, or struggling through the hardest levels of a video game.

'That was … bloody hard work', someone will say, but the underlining sense is: 'Yeah, but we made it!'

Hard fun, unlike soft fun, is *active*. It's challenging. And, by now you're seeing the parallels—hard fun is very much like well-designed work.

Hard work cannot be infinite

If all people see is a whole lot of hard work ahead of them with no end in sight, they may be uninspired to put in the effort required to make progress in the stuff that matters. This is critically important to the process of change, and is at the very core of making work work—we need to see progress, and that means focusing not on the infinite amount of work to be done, but rather on the milestones to be achieved.

Remember the three lenses of challenge, stimulation and reward? Take the last letter of each word—what does it spell? (It spells 'END'—clever, nay?)

We need to literally *keep the END in mind* when we are crafting the games that make work work. We need to make end points and milestones happen sooner and more frequently.

Maybe I've spent too much time with my models, and the END thing is a bit of a forced fit—but the concept of milestones, small wins and mini end-points is very important. The best projects and processes help us to accumulate small wins (and experience the sense of progress that accompanies them) in whatever work we do.

It all relates to the third theory of fun.

Simply put: fun equals tension plus release.

If you've ever played a game of sport, cooked a complex meal, completed a stage in a video game, submitted a big report on time, delivered a kick-ass keynote, run a marathon, jumped from a plane, sumo-wrestled a bear, sat an exam, built a treehouse, launched a product or written a book ... you've experienced the fun of tension (work) and release. These activities might be frustratingly difficult when you're in the thick of them, but the release makes it all worthwhile. It gives you a chance to reflect on what has been achieved (amplifying and reinforcing your sense of progress and mastery).

LEVELLING UP

In traditional Japanese martial arts there used to be only two belt grades — a white belt for 'beginners' and a black belt for 'masters'. It would take someone around ten years of hard, dedicated work to earn a black belt, and some schools and styles still operate this way.

But then the US Marines came along and thought 'stuff that for a joke'. And so they developed a coloured belt system to scaffold the gap between white belt and black belt: a yellow, green, blue and red belt were added. By breaking down the complex process of mastery into proximal goals that focused on the right techniques at the right time, the marines were able to obtain levels of mastery in a fraction of the time.

The focus applied at each belt level also helped keep the marines in a state of flow, ensuring that the lessons learned were never too simple (and boring) for their skill level, or too complex and dangerous for their ability. In other words, a white belt does not attempt a flying dragon kick or a *hadouken*, unless they want to get hurt!

Safe fails

I've only ever dabbled in martial arts — just a few beginner lessons. Interestingly, most of what I learned in aikido and ninjitsu was simply how to *fall* well (as in, literally fall over). I'd like to get a tad metaphorical here and suggest that learning how to fail, and how to fail *safe,* is a key part of any good progress design.

Video games do this well — they make engaging in challenges *safe*, and they make it easy to recover after failure. A video game console won't self-destruct if you fail a mission and die, and you certainly won't get hurt. There are consequences, but these are minimal compared with what may happen in the real world.

Creating environments where it is safe to fail means one can fail *fast*, fail *smart* and fail *forward.*

This is critical in any innovation process, as ideas move from ideation through prototyping to implementation. A good facilitator can make the ideation process safe and effective. Rapid prototyping can help get people failing faster (and getting failures identified and fixed early), and appropriate piloting of new products or processes with the right people can move things forward through implementation. Effectively, you begin the process with a high tolerance for failure, which tapers away as you scale up execution.

An inherent bias to action

Most roleplaying games have an 'experience point' system, represented as a progress bar. Collect enough experience points, and your character will 'level up', unlocking access to new skills, talents and items. As you level up you begin to see your character mastering particular skills and talents — but here's the thing: you only get experience points by engaging in *challenging* work. If you sit around picking daisies all day, you won't be levelling up in a hurry.

The more challenging the task in relation to your skill, the more experience points you get and the more you level up (enabling you to consolidate skills and tackle even bigger challenges). This structure creates an inherent bias to

(continued)

action—an urgent optimism to do great work outside your comfort zone. In many instances you are able to calibrate the level of challenge too. Some people are happy to 'grind' away on low-challenge activities, essentially farming experience the slow way. Others plunge right into things, riding extremes of adrenaline and anxiety in order to progress faster.

Either way, this works because of the *structure* providing visibility of progress, within the context of meaningful, self-calibrated challenge. And this is something that can be created in the real world.

The quantified self

Advances in technology are making it increasingly easy to track things like health, fitness, finances, productivity and movement. This, in turn, gives you visibility of progress (and from there, the ability to set milestones, calibrate challenge and level up). There's a term for this—the 'quantified self'.

Anyone with a smartphone can begin to use it to track data on many aspects of their daily life. (Indeed, there are now sensors you can wear on your head that will allow you to track mental performance and patterns, and even remotely control simple objects with your thoughts—crazy, right?) I've used my phone and special scales to track my weight and lean (or is it fat?) mass. I've also tracked activity and heart rate, used my phone camera (and an app) to track my nutrition and diet, and used my phone to monitor sleep patterns.

Indeed, there is even an app that allows you to track sexual performance in bed. It uses the vibrations of the mattress to track duration, frequency and intensity. It's very popular in the Netherlands, and has a single player mode too (so I hear). Even better, you can share your results on Facebook! Gives a whole new meaning to poking, eh?

Silliness aside, the ability to acquire a heap of data, visualise it and then cross-reference it can empower people to discover meaningful correlations. Notice you're often fatigued and grumpy on Thursday afternoons? Maybe that meeting for pancakes with Sally every Thursday isn't doing you any favours. Notice your sales margin hasn't increased with profits? Maybe it's time to cut back on staff karaoke nights.

You can find a heap of resources at www.quantifiedself.com.

Remember, it all starts by making progress *visible*. We can't lift our game until we know what game we are playing.

Speaking of which, so far we have focused mainly on *finite* games. Games that have end points — the conclusions, small and large, that provide a sense of progress through meaningful challenges.

But all finite games sit within an infinite context.

A vision of play and possibility

The philosopher James Carse says there are at least two kinds of games—one finite, the other infinite. 'A finite game is played for the purpose of winning, an infinite game for the purpose of continuing the play', he writes.

Carse's book *Finite and Infinite Games* is phenomenal. In it he unpacks a deep and rich philosophy of play and possibility. I'll do my best to summarise the gist in the least clumsy way possible, though I do warn you: I'm about to flex the 'Ph' in the PhD I earned a while ago. I relish this, though I'm not the best at it (and I highly recommend you read *Finite and Infinite Games* thoroughly—it's pretty much the number one book I recommend to everyone).

Finite games

Finite games are played for the purpose of winning. A finite game has a precise beginning, and comes to a definitive end once the game is 'won' by a player or team. Winning can occur only when there is agreement from the players, and winning occurs within the context of the rules.

Finite games often have clear spatial and numerical boundaries. Think of a game of football—within the boundary lines a finite game is at play. Different rules operate within this space. These rules are published prior to the play, and all of the players must agree to them before the play begins—this forms the ultimate validation of the game. The rules cannot be changed during the course of the game—in other words, you cannot simply 'make it up as you go'.

And it's here that we find the most critical distinction between finite and infinite play: the rules of an infinite game *must* change the course of play. The rules are changed when the players of an infinite game agree that the play is imperilled by a finite outcome.

Infinite games

So the best way to think of infinite games is in terms of *purpose, mastery, autonomy* and *progress*. These are not fixed outcomes—in fact, in many ways they are asymptotic. There's always more. The big motivation gap and constructive discontent are always there, because there is always more to aspire to. One can achieve 'success' in a finite game, but can only *progress* in an infinite game.

Once you have 'succeeded' the finite game stops, so it is the imperative of the infinite player to change the rules to keep it going. An infinite game has no winner and has no end. The only goal is to keep playing.

Play? You can't be serious!

An argument *against* play is that we need to take things seriously instead. But to be playful is *not* to act as though nothing of consequence will happen. Rather, when we are playful we relate as free and authentic persons, where *everything* that happens is of consequence. 'In fact', Carse argues, 'it is being serious that closes itself to consequence, for seriousness is the dread of the unpredictable outcome of open possibility'. To be serious is to set a specified outcome (like a smart goal); to be playful is to allow for possibility (whatever the cost to oneself).

---

*'Finite players play **within** boundaries, infinite players play **with** boundaries.'*—James Carse

---

Being able to step into, and out of, finite games is a key component of the game changer. Just as the coach of a sports team is able to be both in and out of the game, we need to be able to play finite games well, but within the context of an infinite game.

And now, padawan, you are ready...

The game changer model

Keeping in mind the big gap of constructive discontent we covered in chapter 3, the progress principle of chapter 4 and the anatomy of games (and their parallels to modern insight in motivation) from chapter 5, the *game changer* model in figure 6.1 (overleaf) depicts the process of making change happen, in the context of finite and infinite games.

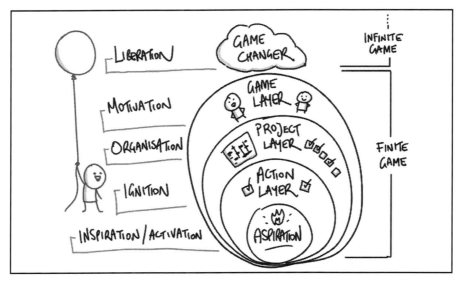

Figure 6.1: the game changer model

Start with the spark

At its strongest, the spark is aspiration, and at its simplest we have the glowing ember of automation. The spark represents the core goal, idea, aspiration or intent that precedes action. It may simply be the vaguely conscious intent to 'show up and do your job'. Or it may be the aspiration to do something better, or new. In any event, the core component of the game changer model is the will of the player.

But noble goals, good ideas and sound intent don't change anything—simply *willing* a thing to happen will not make it so. Remember, *great work* is the not-so-secret secret to success.

So to bring change, progress and growth into existence, we need to *act*.

The action layer

I recently indulged in a mild and well-mannered, er, 'beverage game' after a conference with a number of thought leaders and speaker friends. The rules for the game were quite simple: make increasingly obscure and succinct 'toasts' to the group. 'May your pencils remain sharp with leads unbroken!' is an example of a toast. Another: 'May all your handshakes be long and firm!' And so when it came to my turn, I couldn't help but share the following toast: 'May all your actions be crisp and tickable!' (Actually I didn't say that—I rambled out something useless, but had I had my wits about me, this is what I would have said.)

Because this is where most ideas, goals and intentions don't translate. People talk the good talk, dream big, 'visualise success' and do all that fluff…but it's only when we start to take action that we see progress. And many people are terrible at capturing action steps.

Remember that every idea, aspiration or goal is secretly a whole heap of work in disguise. If you want to make stuff happen, you need to embark upon a series of actionable steps.

Sometimes this is quite simple. If you aspire to visit your favourite local cafe today for that lovely single-origin pour-over and maybe a slice of pecan pie, you simply go to the cafe and make your order. There is no need to work up a fancy Gantt chart. If you aspire to read a particular book, go get that book and read it. Many finite games start and end with a few simple actions.

But often it's not that simple. The reality is that bridging the gap between where we are and where we want to be involves an incredibly complex and variable set of actions. Particularly in organisations.

Simply listing all of the things that need to be done to make change and progress happen is a good idea (I call it a 'task dump')—but remember, much of your strategy and process will *emerge* through the actions you take and the experiments you conduct.

Many people think that once we have a set of tasks listed, we should allocate a priority level to each task. In my experience, this only produces a list with a lot of medium- to high-priority tasks, which isn't too helpful. Too many high-priority tasks can make progress seem too difficult to achieve.

Instead, we need a level of *organisation* to the actions—so we can invest our efforts into the right actions, at the right time and in the right way.

The project layer

Peter Sheahan, author of *Making It Happen* and other great books, argues that *freedom follows focus*. It's kind of like how action precedes clarity. And it's true—you can't do everything all at once.

Freedom follows focus, but *sequence* gives you the freedom to focus.

And that's what the project layer does. It's the organisational layer that makes work *work*. It's where we take all of the action steps, and begin to place them into logical sequences, stages and streams.

Many individuals are bad at translating ideas into crisp action steps, but it can be even worse in organisations. Some still use outdated, top-heavy and cumbersome approaches to organising the work that makes progress happen. Meetings with no action steps, clunky and complex project management software, and layers of bureaucracy. But this is changing.

Scott Belsky, author of *Making Ideas Happen*, argues that it's often the lack of organisation that stops great ideas from happening. When done well, a good project layer provides the structure that makes stuff happen. A good project layer will provide visibility of progress and the stuff that matters, giving people a sense of certainty while keeping entropy at bay.

In chapter 8 we'll unpack the concept of contextual momentum, and explore some effective ways you can go about managing the project layer.

Most motivational challenges can be solved at this level. People generally *want* to do good, meaningful work. Provided that their base compensation is fair, people want to engage in well-designed work.

The project layer and the game layer are very closely connected. A project is, after all, a game. It has goals, rules and feedback. But sometimes the motivation and behaviour within a project can still be misaligned to the bigger strategy. Sometimes the strategy will call for more creative collaboration, and yet the culture still persists as a competitive one.

It's here we need to ascend to the game layer.

The game layer

Where the project layer is largely concerned with organisation, it's the game layer that's concerned with motivation. And really, if you've got the preceding elements right, this is the final 20 per cent. The difference between good work and *great* work.

Here we look at the other elements of goals, rules and feedback often missed in the project layer. Things like the narrative and larger sense of purpose attached to the project goals. The calibration of the level of challenge, and the construction of the rules that shape experience. It's here we play with elements that tap into optimistic urgency and our bias to completion. It's here we make work more *gameful.*

And at this stage, when done well, we'll have crafted a finite game that works.

We step into and out of many different games throughout the course of each day. From the game of making breakfast and getting to work safely, to the little meeting games at work, to the game of progressing the projects that matter. Some games benefit from clear boundaries, although the lines are becoming ever more blurred now as many of us can literally do most of our work anywhere. Have you found yourself checking and answering email outside of work? It used to be that we could simply leave work *at* work. But now, work is no longer a place—it's a state of mind.

Which makes it ever more important to be aware of the many finite games you are playing so you can rise above them, to lift your game and change the game, so everyone is playing a better game.

The game changer

And it's here we cross the threshold, from a finite game to an infinite one. Like zooming out of a map on Google Earth, from street level to planet level, here we zoom out from *within* any of the finite games at play—into something much more meta.

And it's from this space we can change the game.

Here's a little thought experiment to put this into context. Right now, I'd like you to think about what you're thinking about. Yes, that's right, as you read this—think about whatever you're thinking about. Good? Right, you're in a state of metacognition. Which is great. Stay in the moment though, if you can. Because now I'd like you to *see* yourself thinking about what you're thinking about. As though you are zoomed out, looking over your own shoulder. With me? If you are, you're now in a state of doubly dissociated metacognition.

Now I'd like you to imagine that *the real you* is currently at home *playing the current you* as part of a massively multiplayer real-world game. You are in the real world right now and *completely* in control, and you are surrounded by the avatars of other players. But the real you is removed from the current context, and can see things from the game-changer layer (see figure 6.2, overleaf).

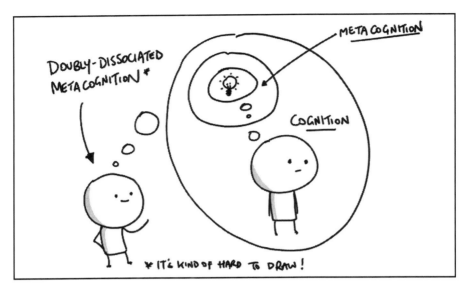
Figure 6.2: doubly dissociated metacognition

Unlike in video games, your experience points, skills and abilities aren't immediately apparent. The quests and missions that'll move you forward aren't immediately apparent. And meaningful feedback on progress is not quite as fast as you experience in a game — but it's all still there. You are still playing these games and you are still totally in control.

Okay, you can stop thinking about what you're thinking about, if you like. But this is still a space that's accessible to you or your team at any time.

Having an argument with a teammate? Zoom out to the infinite game and see what this is really about. Are you contributing to progress, or are you just trying to win and be right?

Not sure why your project seems out of alignment? Zoom out and reassess how the game is working. Run a diagnostic — what needs to change to make it right?

We need *to change the game.*

And often too, if we want to stay ahead of the game.

Business consultant Alan Weiss once said, 'I'm often amazed by how stupid I was two weeks ago'. For me, it's more like two *hours* ago.

The world is changing fast. You, and your team, are learning in the process. The more you do, experiment and explore, the more you learn. And as a result, the wiser you get, which sometimes means *goals* need to shift and adapt.

And the *rules*, well, they aren't fixed. There's no rule that says you *must* follow the rules — or else there'd have to be a rule that says you must follow *that* rule, and so on. Rules are made to *support* progress, not hinder it. If rules are getting in the way of progress for no legitimate reason, they need to be *remade*.

And the *feedback* is what informs. It's the root of all game-changing hacks. Knowledge is power, and we need to empower ourselves and our team with the ability to access a clear sense of progress wherever possible.

CHAPTER SUMMARY

You're at a good level. Now that you know the distinctions between internal, extrinsic and inherent motivation, and how the process of change works, the game changer model introduced in this chapter has put aspirations, actions, projects and all the elements of games in their context, providing you with a new avenue to approach change.

We got a bit philosophical, exploring the concept of fun and the distinction between finite games and infinite games.

Finite games have a start and an end point. They are designed to have winners and losers, success and failure.

Infinite games have no start or end. And they are non-winnable. In an infinite game, the goal is not success, it's *progress* and continued play.

The infinite game correlates to the top layer of the game changer model. It is the space we step into in order to achieve metadissociation from finite games (like stepping from a player's perspective on the field, to a coach's perspective from the sidelines). From this perspective, we can change the games, and get the elements right so that we can progress.

This will all serve you in Part III, where we look at lifting your own game, and shifting work.

PART III ▶

CHANGING THE GAME

LIFT YOUR GAME

We all make choices, but in the end, our choices make us.

—Andrew Ryan

Mahatma Gandhi once said that *we must be the change we wish to see in the world.* I agree—before we go messing around with the game for others, we need to lift our own game.

I say this because it's so much easier to make recommendations on what others should do to solve their problems. It gets harder when we're dealing with our own challenges. This is partly because we can be objective about others. We can see the bigger picture and offer advice from a different perspective. In other words, we can help them *find the game changer*—because we're not *in* their game. We're outside their finite game layer. We're on the sidelines watching.

It's so much harder when you're on the field. Here, it's so much easier to self-sabotage and get in our own way.

Overcoming self-sabotage

The smarter you are, the more likely you are to insidiously sabotage your own progress.

Sabotage is actually pretty cool, as a concept. Saboteurs infiltrate enemy lines, working under the radar to cause all sorts of mischief to hobble the enemy's chance of achieving their objectives. Things like hampering communication, disrupting supply chains, poisoning the wells, hacking through control systems, and so on.

And that's exactly what we do to our own progress, often without even realising it. The gap between where we are and where we want to be is already filled with obstacles and friction, and yet many of us will go on to make it even harder for ourselves to achieve.

We are profoundly adept at getting in our own way.

In eighteenth-century France there was a man by the name of Alexandre Deschapelles. He was a chess master, and he won a hell of a lot of games of chess. Deschapelles was particularly famous for starting a game with one less piece than his opponent; he would literally remove one of the pawns, thereby playing at a significant disadvantage. Despite the handicap he would still win almost every game—even against some of the world's top players.

The few times he lost, though, he would say something along the lines of 'You didn't really beat me. If this was a real game, if I wasn't playing with a handicap, then of course I would have won [twirls moustache]'.

He had an in-built alibi that excused him when he performed poorly.

And that's what we tend to do when we don't get our own game right. When the path to progress is unclear or our goals are seemingly unachievable, many of us will conjure up self-sabotaging stories to excuse our lack of progress and performance.

Think of it like this. You're reading this book right now. Your eyes are picking up characters that strike your retina because of light waves bouncing off the page. If you're hearing anything right now it's because sound waves are bouncing off the walls and stimulating the cilia in your ears. All of these stimuli are being turned into chemical-electrical signals, which are then being converted into meaning by your brain. And also, all matter is purely energy condensed to a slow vibration. We are adrift in a sea of energy that exists at various levels of vibration, making meaning out of stuff.

Metaphysics aside, what we are left with is a choice: make reality mean something constructive, or make it mean something less so. I've tried to capture this in figure 7.1.

Figure 7.1: the malleable reality

Of course it's much more complicated than this. But at a useful level, we can think of it like this: stuff happens, and we make stories around the experience. These stories can support progress, or they may nest an alibi that allows us to sabotage our progress. 'I work better when I'm under pressure' is the classic procrastination story to explain why things are always left to the last minute. 'There just wasn't enough time', says the perfectionist who invests a disproportionate amount in beginning a task and so runs out of time to complete it.

These stories thrive on vagueness and an unclear game. They fall apart when we create real visibility of progress.

Essentially we need to make it hard to make it hard for ourselves.

We are about to look at each of the most common forms of self-sabotage, the stories we tell ourselves, and the effect it has on our motivation and behaviour.

We'll also look at how we can change the game in each situation, hacking our own motivation to make better progress.

If you refer back to the game changer model (p.132), you'll see in almost every instance it's like running a diagnostic through each layer:

- establishing a goal, aspiration, or sense of meaning, relevance or purpose
- identifying the actions that can be undertaken to make progress
- seeing what's getting in the way, or what needs to be arranged in order to simplify complexity and make progress visible
- calibrating the challenge and tweaking any other elements (triggers, rules, stimulation, feedback and so on) to get the game right.

And so, we've waited long enough — to put it off any further would just be ironic. Let's look at procrastination, that dastardly larrikin that often gets in the way of progress.

Making procrastination work

Procrastination. We all do it, and many of us think it's the enemy. And yet, procrastination is often the result of our behaviour defaulting to activities that give us the richest sense of progress.

When tackling procrastination, the biggest wins are achieved not necessarily by eliminating access to the activities we procrastinate over (that only enhances craving anyway), but rather by making it easier to see progress in the activities that matter.

So, let's unpack procrastination.

The story: 'I work better when I'm under pressure.'

The sabotage: We allow ourselves to get distracted, delaying important work until the last minute. This enhances the pressure we experience, and the risk that things may go wrong.

The alibi: If things don't go well, we can always say, 'I didn't have enough time'. If you happen to become unwell in the crucial last hours, or if your computer breaks down, even better—you can blame it on that.

Now, here are a few ways you can change the game to make procrastination work.

Literally make procrastination work

Make the things you procrastinate on the very things that contribute to progress. In other words, surround yourself with progress-making tasks.

I used to show university students how to enjoy exams. Part of this meant establishing study environments where you combine a primary task (that is, the one in front of you) with two peripheral tasks (one either side of you). For example, you might have economics study to do in front of you, a history assignment to the left, and a maths assignment to the right.

By mixing up the types of thinking required for each 'zone' (emotive/creative and logical/analytical), your three work zones essentially allow you to channel-surf; when your mind wanders, it has a productive place to land.

Track yourself

There are some great software applications that help you to track where your time is invested each day on the computer, but I find it's a combination of both digital and analogue tracking that works best.

Just like keeping a food diary, a time diary will make you extra conscious of where your time is being invested. You'll have a clearer sense of the game you are playing, and, as we covered in chapter 5, the Hawthorne Effect may see your performance naturally increase simply because it is being monitored.

By having data to play with, you can pick up on patterns of behaviour, and you'll be better placed to calibrate your game.

Craft your own 'last minute'

Author Rita Mae Brown once quipped, 'If it weren't for the last minute, nothing would get done'. But the fact that there even *is* a 'last minute' implies there is a structure — a deadline — which means there's a start point and a gap in between. In other words, a game we can tweak. Remember how we discussed crafting 'end points' in chapter 6? That's what we need to do here. We need to make that last-minute come sooner, to manufacture our own sense of urgency. At its simplest, it looks like this:

- Make a list of all of the discrete tasks associated with progress.

- Arrange this list into a logical sequence.

- Break down the immediate (proximal) tasks into smaller subtasks (ensuring that each subtask can be completed in around 15 minutes).

- Establish mini-sprints of work — try to knock off five subtasks in under an hour.

- Maintain clear visibility of progress throughout.

Visibility precedes accountability. If you want to be accountable for your actions, make your action steps visible first.

Structure-casting

In the early stages of writing this book, I made a bold declaration that I would post daily video updates on progress to my friends on Facebook. I declared this to the thousands of subscribers of my museletter, inviting them to friend me on Facebook and watch. It was something ridiculous like 50 000 words in 50 days, with mini-goals of 1000 words each day.

It sure got me moving, knowing I had to upload a video post each day to comment on progress. Did I miss days? Sure. My work involves a heck of a lot of flying between countries, and deep immersion with clients. Did I miss targets? You bet. But did the structure help facilitate progress and stave off procrastination? Definitely.

Procrastination often occurs when we have a purpose but no process. If you've ever felt that pure goal setting isn't the bee's knees, then structure-casting is something you might love. It adds more of the rules and feedback of games to the goals you've got.

Remember, our motivation and behaviour will always default to activities that provide the richest sense of progress. We show up and go to work, because there is a structure in place (a game). If you play sport, the structure and accountability inherent in the game will serve to keep you committed. If you're learning a musical instrument or are enrolled in a course of any kind — again, the structure serves you.

I used to coach senior students in exam performance. In some of the elite schools I worked with, students would struggle to find time for study — between attending school, participating in sports training and weekly matches, their part-time jobs and other extracurricular activities, there just isn't much time left for study. Or so they say.

What is really happening is that the limited time they do have is being absorbed by the activities with the clearest structures. With sport, you are accountable to your team. You have a timetable and clear expectations. The same with school, and work. But with study, ah... there's a game that's barely designed at all.

This is an important point. When it comes to our own projects, our motivation often wanes (in spite of clear goals) because of the *lack* of structure.

So, we need to structure-cast.

When structure-casting, rather than simply setting a specific goal, you cast out a structure into the future. I say 'cast' quite deliberately because (a) it's wizard-like, and that appeals to me, and (b) if you imagine it like a fishing rod, you'll get that it's all about investing a small amount of effort into a structure that will allow you to reel yourself towards your goal. It's something you can do easily, too. Keeping it 'reel', so to speak.

Here are five simple components of a good structure-cast:

1. **Make a bold declarative statement** about what you are in the process of achieving. Avoid non-bold statements like 'I'm going to' or 'I'm aiming to'. Say it like it already *is*, but focus on the *doing* ('I'm writing a book' is better than 'I'm going to write a best-selling book').

2. **Time-bracket it.** Craft an end point to it — set a date. The compression of time enhances the challenge and focus of the project, and makes it less likely it will fall victim to other priorities.

3. **Choose a platform** that gives you great progress visibility. I chose Facebook for my early quest, but you might choose a visible chart in your office (where people can see it). Make it hard to hide progress (in other words, make it easy for you and others to see the game you are playing).

4. **Embrace cognitive dissonance.** When your actions match your words, you've got congruence. But when you make a bold declaration, and your actions don't yet match it, you've got cognitive dissonance. At this point, you'll naturally seek to close this dissonance either by taking actions (congruent to your words), or by reframing the original statement by succumbing to self-sabotage. To prevent reframing from happening, you need to...

5. **Track data.** The qualitative elements of a bold statement are all well and good, but you'll also need to incorporate objective measures to get a true assessment of progress. This can take many forms — from a daily check box, to a word count or a fancy line graph. Remember: progress motivates, so make sure the structure you cast has good mechanisms to assess your progress.

The right structure (or, more specifically, greater clarity on the rules and feedback) can help you reel yourself out of procrastination.

But sometimes you've just got to take a good hard look in the mirror, roll up your sleeves and say 'when in Rome'.

Organise your own productivity blitz

I got the concept of a 'productivity blitz' from my good mate, author and thought leader Matt Church. It's like summoning all of the power of the last minute, but on your own terms. Choosing your own battleground.

If you know you have a tendency to get distracted and disrupted on the path to progressing important work, sometimes you've just got to craft out the right space for it. This is where you achieve an epic amount of work in a short amount of time.

As I mentioned, my work has me doing a heck of a lot of flying—which is a nicely contained opportunity for a productivity blitz. As soon as the seatbelt light goes off and I'm able to use electronic devices, it's game on. The laptop comes out and I crunch away at work until the battery dies, the person in front of me lowers their seat ('Bastard!' I think, but I'm too nice to say anything) or the plane lands.

But some people don't need to fly that often (trust me, you get over it). If that's the case, you can craft your own productivity blitz. All you need is:

- a start and end point (usually no more than 36 hours)
- a productive space.

The space bit is key. You need to manage two things:

- **The ability to distract yourself**—For some, this means cutting themselves off from the internet. For others, it means leaving the home environment to head to a caravan park for a few days.
- **The ability of others to distract you**—Your friends and family sometimes won't understand the struggle you're in, and will tempt you with a barrage of little activities and opportunities to avoid doing the work. By removing yourself from the source of distractions, you can create a space that is more conducive to getting stuff done.

If you are going on a retreat for a productivity blitz, make sure you have all of the elements that will support you. Good coffee and wine are a good start.

But if all else fails, blackmail yourself to victory

Aherk.com is an online self-blackmailing service. It works using three simple steps:

1. Define a goal and set a clear deadline (again, crafting a container).
2. 'Put your ass on the line.' Upload a compromising picture of yourself. Like that one time, when that donkey...Okay, we won't go there, but in any event

find a photo you don't want people to see. That photo will be posted on your Facebook wall if you fail to achieve your goal.

3. Your friends decide. After your deadline expires, your Facebook friends will vote to determine whether or not you achieved your goal.

This relies on a few things: that you have good friends who respect the integrity of the game and the intention behind it, and that the picture you upload is so bad that you are compelled to complete the task.

This concept can, of course, be replicated without Aherk and Facebook. You can blackmail yourself, or reward yourself, at any time.

But did you notice something here? This is the first time we've mentioned an *extrinsic* motivator. You can do the flip side, of course, and whitemail yourself with a reward. And you know what? At this point in the game, rewards are okay. Why? Because they narrow focus, and if procrastination (the over-widening of your focus) is preventing you from progressing, by all means hack the structures to set things straight. Just don't get too carried away with it! I remember once rewarding myself with chocolate for every chapter edited. Suffice to say I've still got some working out to do.

Perfecting perfectionism

So hey, are you a perfectionist?

The correct answer for all of us is: 'at times'. But it's a worry when this becomes 'most of the time'. Especially when it gets in the way of progress.

A perfectionist will delay action until the environment or context is just right. They won't start until:

- all their emails are done
- their desk is neat, with objects geometrically aligned
- they have all the information
- they've thought it through and planned it properly
- the typography is all in alignment
- their pencils are sharpened
- [insert literally anything].

And they won't be ready to ship until:

- their work meets their ridiculously high standards
- the last possible minute, or later.

I sometimes think of the various forms of self-sabotage as demigods who like to drop in on what we're doing. Procrastination is the vanilla version. And perfectionism is the richer, older sibling.

I'm a good friend of perfectionism. Perfectionism comes to visit for a cup of tea quite regularly and I never get anything done when she is around. When she's over, I find myself spending a lot of time working on minor details — fonts and alignment, getting the colours just right, and getting the first few words of every new paragraph just perfect... [days pass]. So, let's unpack perfectionism.

The story: 'There just wasn't enough time' or 'I didn't have the right resources'.

The sabotage: Perfectionism is an elite form of procrastination. We get caught up in micro-details, investing a disproportionate amount of time in the initial action steps of a project. Or, we make progress contingent on external factors seemingly beyond our control.

The alibi: The quality of your work will not be in question — just the completeness. But, you can always point to the fact you didn't have all of the right resources, or that the internet went down... and so on.

Before we get too carried away, it's important to realise that each form of self-sabotage has a flip side. Procrastination can contribute to great lateral thinking, for example. And perfectionists usually take pride in their work, and hold themselves to high standards, which is a good thing.

It's only a bad thing when perfectionism gets *in the way* of progress. Or when you become crushed under the weight of your own perfectionism. Indeed, Dr Brené Brown, author of *The Gifts of Imperfection,* suggests that it's not necessarily the relaxing of standards, but rather self-compassion, that is the cure for perfectionism.

So if you are a bit of a perfectionist, or if you have perfectionists on your team, here are some tricks you can deploy (in addition to the activities we discussed in 'Making procrastination work' earlier in this chapter—see p. 144).

Draft stamp it

Everything is a version. Whether it's version 0.1, 0.2, or even version 4.3—things just work to get better and better. Nothing is ever fully done.

For perfectionists, it's important to realise this. 'Perfect' is asymptotic—we'll never actually reach it. But in the meantime we can certainly move things *nearer* to perfect.

Draft stamping means declaring, upfront and early, that what you are submitting is not going to be perfect. And you know it. And you're okay with that—it's just a draft. One of many.

When I worked on this book, I was massively worried by perfectionism. It severely hobbled my progress in many ways. When it came time to submit the manuscript to the wonderful folk at Wiley, I believe I called it a very, *very* rough draft. Somehow, that helped to relieve the anxiety and the not-so-useful belief I had that my writing needed to be 100 per cent perfect, straight away.

And since then I've worked with a wonderful editor to bring things closer to perfect. Is it perfect? No. But unlike the saying 'good enough is good enough', sometimes we just need to accept that very, very good is good enough. It doesn't have to be perfect.

In fact, we should ditch perfectionism in favour of its more useful counterpart—which is progressionism.

Replace perfectionism with progressionism

We should all be progressionists. A progressionist will:

- start before they are ready

- iterate and learn continuously

- move through the inconvenient elements associated with making progress (not just thinking about it or planning for it, but actually doing the work)

- respond to changes quickly

- ship as soon as stuff's ready

- remain in constructive discontent while maintaining a sense of optimistic urgency.

Here's a very scientific formula for you:

[Not done because it's not perfect yet] = Bad Perfectionism

[Next iteration done + getting better] = Good Progressionism

Be happy with done and making things better, rather than not-yet-done and not-yet-perfect.

Do you see what we are doing here? We're bringing things back to the root of all game-changing hacks — *providing a clear sense of progress.* It's the key to liberating yourself from perfectionism. Short-circuiting feedback loops helps you to calibrate your attention and effort.

Writing this book, it got to the point where my perfectionism was so crippling I had to cobble together a spreadsheet on the computer, breaking down each chapter into 'proportions of completeness'. This was represented as a number of coloured squares per chapter (10 squares = 100% complete, 2 squares = 20% complete). The mission at the start of each writing session soon became to bring all chapters to at least 80 per cent. Again, it comes back to *structure* and visibility of progress.

Getting over overcommitment

Are you saying 'no' enough?

If your answer is 'No!' then...well, at least you've made a start.

But it's a good idea to keep that practice going if you want to make epic progress in life. Warren Buffett once said that 'the difference between successful people and very successful people is that very successful people say "no" to almost everything'.

You know I'm not a huge fan of the word *success* (*progress* is better) but that sentiment is one worth following. It works when we have a clear structure—a workable game frame. It fails when we don't.

And as has been said before, being vague is just as bad as...that other thing.

When we are vague about our priorities and the projects that matter, we start to say 'yes' to things we really ought not to. We do this to please, to be validated, or for some other form of currency like recognition or appreciation.

In essence, we overcommit.

Overcommitment is one of the most noble forms of self-sabotage. I do it all the time. You probably do too.

To all outward appearances, you are the hero! The knight in shining armour, riding a white horse or something. With a cape.

But underneath your shining armour and dazzling cape, you're martyring yourself for the cause. But in this case, your cause = other people's priorities. Your currency = their attention/acceptance/validation/whatnot.

Here's overcommitment in a nutshell.

The story: 'There are so many things I need to do, there's just not enough time.'

The sabotage: We let other people's priorities displace our own. Or, we commit to too many goals (and play too many games) at once.

The alibi: If something doesn't work, you can easily point to all of the other things you are committed to doing as justification.

Part of the beauty of overcommitment as a form of self-sabotage is that the alibi is *so pure*. While procrastination lets us say 'there just wasn't enough time', and perfectionism lets us say 'it's just not ready yet', the overcommitted can point to everything they're doing and say, 'Well, what do you expect? Look at what I've been doing. I'm on three boards. I've volunteered for these innovation projects, I'm mentoring three interns and I'm already looking after half of the HR role'.

Overcommitment is just so hard to fault.

So watch out for it. Because not only does it get in the way of your own progress—it erodes the quality and impact of what you do.

So, here are some ideas on how you can lift your game and avoid the traps of overcommitment.

Make 'no' your new default

Plenty of people better qualified than me have written on this topic. Just Google it. But here's the gist: saying no doesn't mean becoming a heartless bastard or an insensitive friend. But if you start with 'no', you'll at least buy yourself some time to consider requests appropriately and avoid the biases inherent within the moment.

Matt Church (author of *Amplifiers*—I mentioned him before) argues that our three most precious treasures are time, money and attention. Saying no gives you a greater ability to protect these valuable resources.

Map out your commitments

Whenever faced with a new potential commitment, just ask yourself where you are going to take time and energy *from* to do this new thing. Your exercise or sleep? Your own projects that matter? Time with people who matter?

It's a tough one, no doubt. And don't kid yourself that you can keep everything in balance—you can't. I certainly don't. Life generally doesn't work like that.

Instead it works like a pie chart. In fact, it helps if you map out all of your commitments and put them into a pie chart. A pie chart must fill to 100 per cent—no more, no less. Whenever you say *yes* to something, you're going to wedge a new piece into this pie chart, which means that either another piece will get dislodged, or that you'll have to trim attention away from other commitments.

Dislodging another piece is good. It's the *trimming* that leads to overcommitment. Because when overcommitment is combined with perfectionism, nothing can truly be trimmed.

Therefore, it's saying 'no' to new slices, or dislodging old slices, that will help you avoid overcommitment. And this comes back to *agility*.

Be agile with your commitments

Stuff changes. Priorities shift. We move through seasons of work, and play different games at different times.

Perhaps you need to do a commitment cleanse? Hit the reset button, and wipe the slate clean. That's what Steve Jobs did when he famously trimmed Apple's product line from hundreds to four. 'I'm as proud of what we *don't* do as I am of what we do', he once said. For Jobs, innovation meant eliminating the unnecessary so the necessary might speak.

Is this all just an elaborate plot to avoid real commitment?

Haha-yes-maybe, but no! Well, it depends. Are we tracking the stuff that matters? You can't lift your game unless you know what game you're playing. It all starts with, and comes back to, a clear sense of progress and understanding the games at play.

Other forms of self-sabotage

Procrastination, perfectionism and overcommitment are the three main ways we can hobble our own productivity and progress. But there are a few more.

'Too busy' for progress

Sometimes people are just 'too busy' to make progress. That's their story anyway. And yet when we look at what makes up most of their busywork, it's checking emails, answering calls, attending meetings, and attending to the relentless noise that ultimately sees them running around in circles. The solution? Enhance the visibility of progress. Play-test new rules, like switching the phone off after work, answering emails at only three times each day, or beginning each day with the most important, mission-critical work.

'I just can't get any work done here'

Other times people complain that their circumstances just don't work. 'It's too noisy to get work done here', 'I'm waiting for X to happen first' or 'I have to do my work at home, but by the time I get home I'm tired from work'. The solution? Change the game! Too noisy? Move, or turn down the noise. Waiting for X to happen? Don't, or make your own X, or find another way to work around X. Need to get work done at home, but find yourself tired at night? Get up earlier instead, and map your productivity to your energy levels.

I get a huge amount of work done in cafes. The white noise of all the conversations around me is like a form of static distraction. Put me in a room that's utterly quiet and I get disturbed by any noise that pierces the serenity. Whereas in a busy cafe, there's just a blanket of noise and it's hard to actually get distracted. The only thing you can do is just home in on the work in front of you.

I also know I'm very productive in the mornings, so I generally try to shape my work day around that, working on the most critical things first, then catching up on emails and meetings in the afternoon.

This comes back to one of the simplest and truest pieces of advice ever:

If something's not working, change something or try something else.

The work, and the environment—these are within our ability to influence.

'But no one told me this was due today'

And finally, some people just don't know what's going on. They miss deadlines, and work on the wrong things at the right time (and vice versa). 'I didn't know we had a meeting today', they say. Scott Belsky, author of *Making Ideas Happen,* argues that a level of organisation is paramount for anyone looking to have an impact. You could be the most creative person in the world, but unless you get your stuff together, you'll have zero impact. Compare this with people who are only moderately creative and yet highly organised — *they're* the ones making an impact.

So how do we overcome a lack of organisation? Do I really need to say it? Perhaps not, but I will — we get organised! And if something is getting in the way of this, if something is preventing us from stepping through the layers of the game changer model, then we need to find the friction and deal with it. Again, this comes back to visibility of progress.

In chapter 8 we'll unpack the concept of *contextual momentum* — a way of organising your efforts across short-term and long-term pursuits. It's the thing that combats all forms of self-sabotage — provided you're willing to invest a small bit of time in getting the motivation strategy and design right.

Solve motivational challenges by asking the right questions

We've covered the components of games (goals, rules, feedback) and their correlation to what intrinsically motivates us (purpose, mastery, autonomy). Now, let's run that as a diagnostic, which you can apply to changing the game to unlock the motivation within any project or process. Try to view each question from the game-changer level (doubly dissociated metacognition; figure 6.2, p. 136) — sometimes taking pen to paper helps keep you above the game.

Goals

Here are a few questions you can ask yourself to gain greater clarity on the game you're playing and the meaning you're making.

Is this activity worth the investment of my time and energy?

This is the most basic level of assessment you can undertake. When asking this question, consider the alternatives. What is the benefit or cost of doing *nothing*? Is there an alternative activity that better serves?

Be aware of the various contextual games you are playing. Sure, you may not want to do a particular chore at work, but maybe you *do* want to be an effective contributing member of a team, or you *do* want to support the bigger game of providing for your family.

Is the goal too specific, or not specific enough?

Specific goals will narrow your focus. This is good for short-term, formulaic, routine (robot) tasks with predictable outcomes, or for cutting through procrastination. But, if you're looking for a broader focus goal, you may need to incorporate more of a qualitative element, or to state the goal as a challenge-based question: 'How can we...?'

Can I connect my effort to aspiration and/or the contribution to something bigger than myself?

This links to providing a clear sense of progress. We need to *know* that our efforts are making a difference, but we also need to know *what* this difference we're making is, and *why* we're making it. This links back to the aspiration element we discussed earlier, where inspiration or activation breaks us out of automation (see figure 3.2, p. 50).

Rules

While goals have traditionally held the spotlight of attention from motivation and management alike, the reality is that they can be fairly fuzzy and do not need to be overly thunk. Rules are a bit different. We need rules to make work *work*. Sometimes we've inherited them, but sometimes we need to establish our own rules and rituals around progress.

Are there enough rules to provide the clarity I need to progress towards this goal?

Simplicity is your companion here. Too many rules can hobble progress with bureaucracy. Too few rules can leave people uncertain as to how to move forward.

And while specific goals can hobble creativity, proactively seeking clear rules and constraint can actively *enhance* it (as well as reduce any threats to progress).

Do the rules make things too challenging or not challenging enough? Do they contribute to and allow for mastery?

If a task or activity is becoming too routine and easy, reshape it into a challenge. Try to get twice the amount done in half the time (compression).

If it's too overwhelming, chop it up into smaller pieces, and sequence these pieces logically (calibrate). This will help to keep things in flow, enhancing the likelihood of blissful productivity and progress.

Are the rules relevant to the existing context? Can they be evolved?

Many rules are inherited. They were invented and implemented in a different time, to serve a purpose that may no longer be relevant. It's important to challenge rules that impede progress, and to reshape them into the evolving context.

Are the rules agreeable and understandable to someone other than yourself?

Video games rely on code to manage the rules of the game. In most other games, we just have The Code. Or the agreement between players, or with yourself, about how you will conduct and play the game. The more people are aware of your game, and the easier it is to understand, the more easily they (and you) will be able to hold you to account for your efforts.

Feedback

And here we are, at the root of all game-changing hacks. It starts with, and comes back to, a clear sense of progress. It's what sits in the Big Motivation Gap, if we can but see it. Here are some questions you can ask to test the feedback element of the games you are playing.

Is the latency between effort and meaningful feedback high or low?

The lower the latency, the shorter the delay between effort and meaningful feedback, the more likely you are to sustain continued effort and investment.

Do you have objective quantitative data to work with?

Numbers don't lie and often provide the least ambiguous sense of progress. And numbers are so easy to track—simply put a progress bar on any activity (a start point, an end point and some milestones in between) and you'll already be enhancing quantitative feedback. But you should not rely on numbers alone.

Do you have subjective qualitative data to play with?

While words can get warped, qualitative feedback helps to fill in the gaps between quantitative feedback. This type of feedback also contextualises progress within a bigger picture.

And the critical question: is progress visible?

I mean, is it super easy to access, interpret and see? Many people bury progress under too many layers. It's hidden away in a book, or in folders within folders on a computer, only to be revealed in the occasional meeting or event.

You'll want to make your progress utterly easy to see. Like a cook reaching for their key tools (rather than rummaging through the cupboard), you'll want to be able to retrieve your progress structures (lists, Gantt charts, progress maps...) quickly and easily. And then you'll want to minimise the cognitive effort required to process and interpret the data.

In other words, don't bury progress in reports on computers, and don't wrap it up in words and waffle. Smarten it down into something beautiful.

CHAPTER SUMMARY

In this chapter, we've taken a look at our own progress through the lens of the game changer. We are all profoundly adept at getting in our own way and sabotaging our ability to progress the stuff that matters. We usually do this when the game isn't working, or when something is out of alignment.

Self-sabotage manifests in a variety of ways — procrastination, perfectionism, overcommitment, and so on. Usually, we're not conscious of our own self-sabotage, and we'll have stories that excuse our poor performance.

The path to liberating yourself from any form of self-sabotage starts with visibility. We can't lift our game unless we know what game we're playing.

And so, we ask questions. We review the core components of all games — the goals, rules and feedback. And then we calibrate, tweak, play-test and refine new approaches until we find the game-changing element that works.

By working on the art of liberating ourselves from our own poorly designed work, we're better placed to start working on the bigger stuff.

CHANGE THE GAME

If you do not change direction, you may end up where you are heading.

—Lao Tzu

Well look how far we've come—and we've barely scratched the surface of organisational culture change! 'What gives?' I hear you *not* ask. 'I thought this book was going to give me the secret quick fixes to overnight organisational culture change!' Good, you've been following.

What we're going to unpack in this chapter is an *approach* you can take to tackle culture change. It's complex, requires multiple strategies and is not something that happens overnight. But it *is* something we can tackle at the motivational level, through better work design.

First up, we need to decide—are we on a mission or a quest?

Missions and quests

The question of mission or quest is quite simple: are we going to progress change within an existing paradigm, or do we need to explore a new one?

Missions

Sometimes you and the team know what needs to be done. You know the outcome that needs to be achieved and the general steps needed to get there. I call this a mission.

In a mission, you are working towards a clear promise.

Most work at the operational level consists of missions. They may be as simple as 'surpass last quarter's sales target' or more complex, like 'migrate all employees onto the new internal communications platform'. Here you are generally moving through mapped territory, and the focus is on shaping the dynamics that turn good work into *great* work.

Quests are different.

Quests

Sometimes you don't know what the outcome looks like—you just know you can't keep doing what you're doing. I call this a quest.

In a quest, you are working from a clear premise.

You are moving through uncharted territory, and the focus is on shaping the dynamics that facilitate productive exploration and progress. Where a mission provides the comfort of relative certainty, a quest is more fraught with peril (failures, setbacks, dead-end pathways). The kinks in the road haven't been ironed out yet. Instead, we need to be more pioneering.

Quests usually begin with a question or a clear challenge that needs to be solved. Getting the motivation strategy right for a quest is a bit different from a mission, but the two are related.

Quests nest missions.

Quests can be placed in the same category as a good vision; missions are what bring visions to life. Sometimes missions can nest mini-quests, but generally speaking a big quest will nest more specific missions. A quest is not a specific destination; for example, 'we're heading west' is a quest, whereas 'we're going to New York' is a mission.

'But what's all this talk about missions and quests about?', you may be wondering. It comes down to how we design the structures, rituals and artefacts around our work.

Rituals and artefacts

All cultures are made up of structures, rituals and artefacts. From the culture of a tribe to that of a whole country, from a sporting team and their fans to a start-up team and its work—culture is scaffolded with structures, rituals and artefacts.

Structures are the rules and other elements that make up the games you play at work. They directly influence the collective behaviour of people. We've talked about this a heap already, so let's look at rituals.

Rituals

Rituals are like 'sacred routines'. They are practised sets of behaviours that happen with a fixed level of regularity. Many rituals aren't deliberate, but the best ones are. Individually, rituals are what keep people on track and in the best state to make progress. A walk followed by a fresh coffee and a read of the paper is for some a morning ritual that primes them for a productive day. In the writing of this book, I established similar rituals to move into a productive space to progress the writing. And yes, they involved coffee.

But rituals are even more critical at the team level. Rituals are the *stitching* that connects people to progress. They are the thread that binds a team together in purpose, and they thrive on real connection. Therefore...

We should meet more often.

Many meetings hold the opportunity to become great progress rituals. They are critical for collaboration, but they don't have the best reputation. Most organisations handle meetings terribly. Jason Fried, co-author of *Rework,* argues that work doesn't happen at work, because of meetings. 'Meetings are just toxic, terrible, poisonous things...' Fried suggests.

But I think meetings are a broken game begging to be made better. And I've got a solution for you: *make your meetings frequent, and short.*

The issue isn't the meetings—it's the *duration* of them, the *delay* between them, and their *relevance* to progress. I could do a three-circle Venn diagram for that, but I think I'll go with a quadrant this time (see figure 8.1).

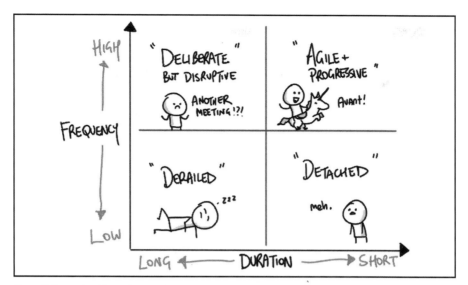

Figure 8.1: we should meet more often

In this model, we contrast two key elements: frequency of meetings (how often), and their duration (how long).

Infrequent long meetings

These seem to be the norm. Issues pile up, and over time those small, easy-to-fix challenges and hiccups become big, hard-to-fix processes and problems. Without the proximal focus of frequent meetings, behavioural issues are left to fester and affect the cultural norms of your team. And because no one likes long meetings, these long infrequent meetings become something to avoid where possible, or to disengage from if you're there. Which only makes meetings worse, perpetuating the cycle. And then, before you know it, a year has gone by and your strategy has derailed. Not ideal.

So yes, let's get rid of those meetings. And while we're at it, let's watch the more frequent long meetings too.

Frequent long meetings

These usually occur at a set time, generally blocked out for a full hour (regardless of the agenda). They're also accompanied by ridiculous formalities like roll calls and minute taking, which are fine for annual board meetings, but in the context of driving growth and improvement they are just unnecessary friction. And you know how we feel about friction.

Frequent, short meetings are where it's at

A seven- to twelve-minute daily or twice-weekly meeting, anchored around a large Gantt chart, 'progress wall' or online road map, is one of the best ways to keep your strategy on track and progressive. Issues can be dealt with as soon as they occur. You create an open ecology, where everything is visible, and there is a bias to action and progress. Risks are mitigated because feedback loops are tight. Good behaviours can be amplified daily. Norms can be shifted. And change can happen.

Daily stand-up meetings are at the core of scrum and agile project methodologies (often used by software developers who work in an incredibly fast-paced industry and deal with change daily). There is a heap of information out there on similar approaches, but you don't need to get too technical.

A FEW GUIDELINES FOR CREATING A DAILY PROGRESS MEETING RITUAL THAT WORKS

Choose an odd time increment to start the meeting, and stick to it

Starting at 9.04 am is much better than starting at 9.00 am, which could easily be interpreted as 'between 9.00 and 9.15' by some of my fellow Gen-Y types. The extra few minutes gives people a chance to get settled and ready.

Set a timer at the start of each meeting

The point of these meetings is to keep them *short*. This means strictly not going over time. Why? Because otherwise the ritual will become a time sink and a burden, impeding progress. The best stand-up meetings should be seven to 12 minutes in duration.

Keep teams small

If your team spans more than a dozen people, and it can't be broken down into smaller units of supervisors, then this level of frequency is not appropriate. Smaller teams consisting of those relevant to the project will keep the meeting burden minimal.

Stand-up meetings work best

Keep people on their feet. This is a team huddle (like I've heard sports teams do), before they go about the challenges of the day. We don't want anyone complacent, any chair hierarchies or any stealth phone-checking. It's a level playing field, and ideally your team will be spread in a circle.

Of course, if your team is remotely dispersed, you can use software to 'hang out' with each other. Ideally, you'll want to *see* each other — it's only seven to 12 minutes, and we want full participation.

Every meeting needs a facilitator

This role can rotate, but it's usually good for the team leader to do this, as they can report briefly on higher level contextual changes. The facilitator's role is to:

1. keep the meeting in flow and to time (One of my clients once had a Nerf gun that shot foam darts at people who spoke over time — they called it 'the silencer'.)

2. contextualise contributions into the bigger picture of progress

3. hold and reinforce the narrative, reminding the team of the bigger game.

Everyone needs to answer two questions:

1. What did you achieve yesterday?

2. What are you working on today?

The goal of this game is not inquiry — it's insight. It's about making visible the work that each individual is doing, and contextualising that into the collective. When each person answers these questions, we create an open ecology — and yes, it is a bit Darwinian. There's nowhere to hide. But this is a good thing, as it means people won't be struggling in silence. With the clients I've helped establish this ritual, teams begin to self-regulate. They rally to support the performance of individuals, which in turn elevates the progress of the team.

Anchor all effort back to the overarching context and your project framework

It's best to do this visibly. I've helped some clients develop a very large 'progress wall' — a big, dynamic visual Gantt chart that maps focus and project dependencies across time. But really, any form of visible progress (a bar chart, a road map, a checklist) works. By having something visual to refer to, everyone will see how their effort plays a part in something significant. You'll directly provide a clear sense of progress. A well-facilitated ritual like this can forge a highly effective team through challenge.

If you're attempting any sort of growth, change or progress: *frequency trumps duration, every time.*

But what if your team can't meet in person, or frequently?

Some teams are dealing with 80 per cent operational work, and change/progress management is only a sliver of their responsibility. Other teams are separated by the tyranny of distance, making face-to-face meetings purely an annual event. In these cases, you'll want to have an online structure. A place for projects (and progress) to live *in between* your less frequent meetings.

A cobbled-together space on your intranet, or a long chain of reply-all emails just isn't going to cut it. This needs to be as frictionless an experience as possible—we want it to be utterly easy for people to access and contribute to.

There are plenty of good cloud-based collaborative project management tools and secure, internal social network apps available to organisations and teams wanting to progress change. And most of them cost less per month per person than the coffee at a physical meeting would cost. If you're serious about driving progress through change, you'll give these a good look.

I should also briefly mention infrequent, short meetings

These meetings could be a good thing if your system is working. If you've got formulaic processes with predictable outcomes, it's great to not have to check in with it too often, and to have it hum along. But if you're driving change, you'll need more frequency.

There are many other rituals within organisations—annual conferences, quarterly reviews, rewards and recognition nights, and the like. Each ritual serves to reinforce a particular set of behaviours that are congruent to strategy and an evolving context.

With solid rituals in place to help drive progress and change, let's discuss the artefacts.

Artefacts

Artefacts are the legacy of meaningful effort, and the landmarks of culture. To put it simply, artefacts are the stuff that reflects the work you do and the collective values your organisation holds.

I should note, I tend to avoid going into axiology—the study of values. It fascinates me deeply, but I'm not really that qualified to comment on this area yet (maybe it'll feature more in the next book). But what I do know is that most of the 'values work' I've seen organisations do is nothing more than superficial fluffery. 'We are committed to innovation, collaboration and excellence in all things'—bah. *What you do* is what you are committed to. And it's what you do that makes up culture. Recall figure 0.1 (p. xix)—motivation precedes behaviour, which collectively forms culture.

A few organisations do this well, though. Valve, the software company we referenced in chapter 2, has its employee handbook—an artefact that directly reflects (and influences) the culture it wants to maintain. And of course, there are the modern torchbearers of work culture, like Zappos.

The inevitable Zappos examples

I once spoke at an event in Chicago where Jenn Lim, the author of *Delivering Happiness* and co-creator and CEO of Zappos (an online shoe and clothing store), also delivered a keynote. I'd often heard about Zappos. Everyone references it when talking about culture, famously quoting how after their five weeks of training, new recruits would be offered more than $4000 to quit. It sounded like a cute story, but when Lim shared that they're constantly having to raise this level because not enough recruits were opting to leave, I began to see how true it was! This is a very powerful structure—a threshold for new initiates to pass if they want to be a part of the Zappos culture.

But it goes beyond this one element. For example, Zappos has a 'Face Game': whenever you log into the intranet the face of a fellow employee pops up. You're asked to enter the person's name, and whether or not you answer correctly, you see a bio and profile. Zappos uses this as a way of getting to know co-workers, keeping everyone connected.

But the main reason I bring up Zappos is because of its primary artefact—the Zappos Family Culture Book. Lim shared that, as Zappos began to grow, two questions became important: How can we sustain this culture? And how can we remember it while simultaneously inspiring ourselves for the next year?

The result was a book, an artefact, that translated the fuzziness of culture into something tangible. It contains a collage of unedited submissions from employees (photos and words) who have shared their ideas about what the Zappos culture and core values mean to them, and a new version is created each year to reflect the true feelings of the culture.

Other structures and artefacts

Behance, the creative company of author Scott Belsky, has what it calls a 'Done! Wall'. Instead of simply throwing away lists of completed action steps, some of the team actually decorates the space with them. The walls are literally plastered with completed projects. 'Why throw away the relics of your achievements when you can create an inspiring monument to getting stuff done?' Belksy asks. 'A "Done! Wall" reminds you that you have moved forward in your journey.'

Speaking of moving forward, let's unpack that contextual momentum model I've hinted at a few times.

Contextual momentum

Here's my attempt to help people and organisations get the balance right between specific goals and open possibilities, while still making progress. I call it *contextual momentum*, and it maps what needs to be kept in mind if you want to drive meaningful progress and change (see figure 8.2).

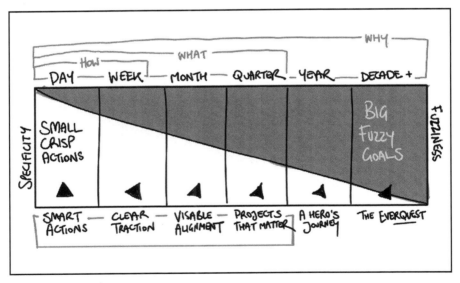

Figure 8.2: contextual momentum

Remember with the game changer model how I said it was akin to zooming out from street level to planet level on Google Earth? Contextual momentum is a bit like that too. But in this case, you're moving through chunks of time — as though you were moving from your daily agenda, to a week page in your planner, to a month view on your calendar, and so on.

It's all about *context*. Years nest quarters, which in turn nest months, then weeks, then days. Your ability to zoom up and down through these layers, while keeping in mind the layers of the game changer model, will help you to manage for the right things at the right level.

The other element in this model is the balance between specificity and fuzziness. For stuff that's proximal (close) to you, we want things to be specific. I was fairly ruthless with SMART goals earlier, in chapter 1 — but at a daily level we do want things to be specific, measurable, achievable, relevant and time-based. We just don't necessarily want that same narrow focus applied with the same intensity to stuff that's way too 'distal from our locus of control' (academic-speak for 'too far away from what we can reasonably influence and control'). So you'll see a balance between big fuzzy distal goals and small crisp proximal actions.

Let's have a look at each layer in more detail.

Crisp daily actions

Actions are what translate ideas, goals and aspirations into reality. Without the *doing* of stuff, nothing gets done, and nothing happens.

Here the focus is on capturing and processing action steps.

May your actions be crisp and tickable!

By crisp, I mean sharp and specific. And by tickable, I mean that it can be ticked off in a checkbox. It can be quickly and clearly assessed as done or not. 'Clean up email' is not crisp and tickable. 'Achieve inbox zero' is.

Here's the anatomy of an action step:

- It starts with a *verb*.
- The middle bit has a *focal point*.
- It ends in an *outcome*.

Remember, fuzziness is the enemy here. At the start of each day, you will ideally have a ritual and a structure to check in with that lets you know (or helps you decipher) what your mission-critical action steps are.

Identify your mission-critical actions

Mission-critical action steps are the things you have identified that, out of all possible things you could be doing, will most likely contribute to meaningful progress. By all means collect other action steps and create a list for your day (it's one of the simplest motivational hacks), but be sure to delineate or highlight the mission-critical actions. Keep these to no more than three per day (any more will dilute the importance of mission-critical actions).

Digital and analogue processing

There are two primary ways you can go about capturing and managing crisp daily actions.

You can go digital and use a task-management application. There are plenty of good ones to choose from, and most offer a free trial period. Make sure it syncs across all of your devices, and if you're working as a team, ensure it syncs up easily between operating systems. You'll want something that provides a blissful, frictionless experience.

Generally speaking, a ruthlessly well designed app with few features will serve you better than a moderately well designed app junked up with features.

The alternative is to go analogue and use a journal or planner. This works for individuals but is tricky to manage among teams, so you may need to take a blended analogue and digital approach here.

But let's focus just on you. If you're the type of person who prefers to write things down rather than type or tap things in, then for goodness' sake make sure the tool you use is one you like using. Invest in one good journal — something big enough to capture and process what needs to be captured and processed, yet compact enough to be with you when you need it. Spreading your action steps across multiple journals increases fuzziness, making it harder for you to be deliberate and to see progress.

Minimise friction and keep things visible

It always comes back to visibility of progress and the minimisation of friction. Make your preferred task-management tool easy to use on a daily level. Have it within easy reach — on your phone, tablet or laptop, or in your bag. Have it easy to get to — a few clicks, taps or page flips and you're where you need to be.

Clear weekly traction

The next level in contextual momentum is the weekly view. It's the default parameter within which many of us view and plan our week, in both digital and paper-based journals.

Here we focus on *traction*, making sure our progress towards completing bigger projects isn't getting derailed. By checking in weekly, and referencing actions to a bigger game, we avoid situations where months later we realise we've gone significantly off track. This works when we have a progress *ritual* based around reviewing the action steps achieved. This may be an extra ten minutes added on to a daily stand-up meeting, or a 20-minute meeting you schedule into your own calendar each week. It may be a Sunday morning thing you do at your favourite cafe.

If you, or your team, are on track, then great! All is good. Celebrate the progress made, and focus on forecasting for the week ahead.

Forecasting

Here is where we reference *up* to the project layer, contextualising our effort over the past week, and using our evolving understanding of the project to calibrate our intended efforts for the week ahead.

Earlier, when discussing the concept of rules, I mentioned how we need to proactively anticipate and seek constraints, so we can proactively prevent or mitigate threats to progress. This is best done at a weekly and monthly level.

If you've looked at the week that's gone by, and you notice that you haven't ticked your mission-critical boxes, it's time to diagnose what's going on.

Friction blasting

If a day goes by and you don't achieve your mission-critical actions, it's not the end of the world. We're only human, and stuff happens — unforeseen externalities and other things beyond our ability to control can get in the way.

But if a week goes by with most of your mission-critical action steps unachieved, then we need to review the game at play. It's here we run through the diagnostic discussed at the end of chapter 7.

Often, the main issue is that the mission-critical action steps are too big, and need to be chopped up a bit more to calibrate the challenge and fit them into the flow of each day. Sometimes, unforeseen friction exists between you and the action—but by making an honest attempt to carry out these actions, and by having a progress ritual to review each week, you are better informed and able to blast away the friction that gets in the way of traction. This is working with *agility*, like a ninja-scientist.

Which then brings us to the monthly level of perspective.

Visible monthly alignment

The monthly level of perspective within the contextual momentum model sits between two important levels of focus—the *task*-based and *project*-based. Here we see the need for things to be much less specific than you'd want to see at a daily level (though still more specific than what's needed at a yearly level). To ensure that your activities and efforts are aligned with the greater project, we need to both set and check against what that alignment will be.

All projects move through phases and stages.

Classic platform video games see characters move through a number of stages, sometimes through different worlds (underwater, in the sky, underground, and so on). Projects can be very much like this—we move through distinctly different phases.

Quests move through phases, such as:

- *diagnosing* the real challenge, challenging assumptions, taking stock and doing environmental scans to know the landscape—asking the right questions to identify what's really going on
- *generating* ideas and establishing creative hypotheses to test
- *refining* ideas and rapidly prototyping new approaches through progressive experiments
- *scaling* experiments into larger programs, and working to implement them across an organisation.

Missions also move through similar phases, easily broken down into an overarching project plan.

Being aware of what phase you're in, or what stage you're going through, is incredibly useful for determining the type of motivational dynamic most aligned with progress (more on this soon). To do this, we need to think in terms of *projects*.

Quarterly projects that matter

It's here we begin to encounter a level of time consideration we don't typically see captured by most conventional tools—the quarter. If you ever feel lost in the world of good *busy* work, rather than the world of great *progress-making* work, there's a good chance it has something to do with the tools you use and the limited perspective they bring.

If you have a look at your calendar right now (on the wall, on your phone or desktop—wherever), chances are the default view is monthly, weekly or daily. Is it therefore any wonder we get caught up in the busywork?

After actions, projects are the next critical element

If you recall the game changer model (see figure 6.1, p. 132), the project layer is the layer directly above the action layer. Here, at a quarterly level, you'll need to choose three important projects you want to progress. Just as with your mission-critical actions, you want to choose *three* projects that matter each quarter.

Projects differ from goals in that they are fully contained, finite games—each project has goals (project objectives/deliverables), rules (time, budget and resources) and feedback. And, just as actions are crisp and tickable, projects are things that you ship—they have a clear deliverable, and a clear way of distinguishing between done/shipped and not. Projects are your missions, and they can be ticked.

And finally, just as actions are best captured and processed with a *task* management system; projects are best progressed with a good *project* management system.

Project management systems

Project management is incredibly unsexy in most organisations. It should be awesome, but sometimes the process and the software that supports project management can be a whole lot of hard, clunky work with steep learning curves, junked up with features and a tacky user experience. But managing your projects doesn't have to be like this.

You don't need a background in engineering or qualifications in project management to drive progress. All you need is to manage the *sequence* of action steps, and to provide visibility over progress and the stuff that matters.

At its simplest level, arranging a to-do list into a logical sequence is a form of project management. We just want to take the essence of that approach, and amplify it.

If you're looking at your own projects, you can actually get by with a simple Gantt chart. Now, I love me a good Gantt chart (see figure 8.3). They were named after a chap called Henry Gantt in the early 1900s and designed as a way of mapping project schedules. But before then a Russian chap by the name of Karol Adamiecki had created something very similar. He called it a *harmonogram*—and I quite like that. It sounds harmonious, and that's what a good Gantt chart can be—it can bring harmony in what otherwise might be a chaotic sea of action steps.

Because remember, we're moving up and down through these contextual layers here. And just as executing a series of mission-critical action steps can progress projects, projects provide the contexts that define what action steps are mission critical.

Figure 8.3: a progress map

A Gantt chart can be simply mocked up on a spreadsheet or sketched on a napkin. It could be a light and simple, dedicated cloud-based app you pay for by a monthly subscription. Or it could be an ultracomplex piece of software that gets in the way of progress. When it comes to choosing a project management system, the same advice as for task management systems applies: choose something well designed that errs on the side of simplicity rather than complexity. The primary purpose of your project management system is to keep actions in alignment with progress, and to keep things moving.

Fail 50 per cent of your projects

Peter Cook, author of *The New Rules of Management*, argues that the implementation of projects that matter is the only thing that matters. They are the very things that drive progress. And we should fail 50 per cent of them. And this is brilliant.

Just as video gamers will spend about 80 per cent of their time failing, we'll want to be failing 50 per cent of our projects that matter. (Yes, you read that right.) Why?

Because the opposite of failure is *apathy* (not success). I've heard it said that we should reward success and failure, but punish apathy. By failing something properly, it still means you are *doing* something. You're still exploring methodologies, conducting experiments to find what might work. 'This mindset...helps you *complete* projects', Cook says. He argues that the strategy is to make our failures as cheap, quick, small and private as possible.

Now, don't cheat at failing your own projects. Remember how we talked about suspending disbelief (and belief) until we collect the evidence? Well, don't be too hasty in declaring a project as 'failed' before you're sure you've given it a decent attempt. And even then the failure is more likely to do with the method, not the goal or concept behind the project.

But hey, if it truly sucks then fail it fast and progress to the next approach. Don't tie yourself to a sinking ship. Remember: progression trumps perfection.

Your yearly 'word'

Beyond the focus of 90 days (a quarter), things start to get much fuzzier. It's mighty difficult for us to predict with specific clarity where we'll be in a year's time. Our sense of it will be fuzzy, and that's fine. Fuzzy distal goals still give us a destination to aim for — we just have a lot more room to adapt, evolve and grow along the way.

To avoid the crippling effect of a too-specific goal set too far into the future, I advocate that each year you have a ritual to do three things.

1. Reflect

A yearly retreat, or something that removes you and your team from your normal context, is a great way to reflect on progress made and plan for the year ahead. Individually, you may choose to do this around the end or start of your calendar year (as there are usually a lot of bigger rituals and traditions tied around the summer/winter equinox), but in business you may simply want to choose your quietest times.

Some business functions run hotter than others at different times of the year. Sales teams often have different cycles from HR, for example. Whatever the case, a relatively quiet period in your calendar is a good time for reflection and strategic development.

Shifting context is important, as it helps you to review the game more objectively. When we are reflecting upon our year, a key thing to highlight is the emerging narrative—how has the *story* developed since this time last year?

In chapter 9 we'll unpack the *monomyth*, the underlining story behind every hero's journey, and how it applies to the game at play.

2. Reset

This is also a good time to hit the 'reset' button—when things are quieter, you can invest in bigger development 'upgrades'. Shifting office, updating software platforms, eliminating temporary fixes that have become permanent fixtures. And while it can happen at any time, this is the best time to invest in new structures and rituals, and to develop artefacts that support the behaviours you want to see more of.

3. Reword

Some people choose to reward themselves at least once a year. That's fine, but I suggest you *reword* yourself as well.

Each year, choose one word. One big, contextual word for your year. No resolutions, no smart goals—just one big word that's meaningful for you.

In the year of writing this, the word I chose was *kingly*—I think I may have copied this from blogger and author Chris Brogan. To me, kingly meant things like 'stepping up', 'taking responsibility', 'serving others' and growing a beard (among other things). I have a friend who made their year 'The Year of Vitality' and another who had 'The Year of Style'. The important thing is that these words don't need to mean anything to anyone else—they embody your big fuzzy contextual goal for the year.

The next step is to ensure that at least one of your three projects that matter each quarter is something that will directly contribute to this word. Writing this book is a project that mattered to my kingly quest this year. For my vitality-focused friend, it included projects like cooking classes, running marathons and snowboarding overseas.

At an organisation or team level, you can rally together around one word too. It might be *growth* or *transition* or *discovery* or *service*—whatever is relevant to the emerging context. At this level, it really does not need to get more specific.

And finally, the fuzziest level of all—a decade and beyond.

The lifelong everquest

This is as fuzzy as it gets. If you refer back to the contextual momentum model on p. 172, the very left hand (proximal) side of the model is focused primarily on *what*. What you are going to do, specifically, to move things forward each day.

Here, on the most distal far right, the focus is on *why*. What is your purpose? The epic meaning and legacy you are aspiring to? Everything from a year onwards is distinctly part of an infinite game. There are no boundaries around it. No winning or losing—just continuous play.

If you're not sure what your megavision is, and if you can't find the epic purpose in your work—don't worry. You're on the everquest, and collapsing something so big and important into something tangible would rob it of its meaning. Just stay curious and sceptically optimistic, and keep on the everquest. Your legacy will be the completed projects and progress you leave in your wake.

And that's contextual momentum. Knowing how every action sits within, and contributes to, a bigger context is a key philosophy to embed in your work.

Shaping culture

As discussed earlier, culture is simply a set of behaviours replicated within a given context. *Motivation* is what drives behaviour. *Behaviour* is what you do (whether you're conscious of it or not). And *culture* is the sum of a group's behaviours. It underpins all results.

Culture can be bloody hard to change, and it's not something I'd advise tackling directly—it's far too ethereal. Instead, we need to flank it with science, and tackle the behaviours directly by working on the motivation strategy and design that sits behind them (technical-speak for saying we need to change the game).

Culture change happens at a behavioural level.

The smaller the team, the more open to influence the culture will be.

Some of my clients are among the fastest growing companies in Australia. I remember one particular client fondly recalling the 'good old days' when it was just him and the other three founders, working together in a share house to crack big corporate clients. In the space of two or three years, his boutique consulting firm has scaled up to having over 200 staff. A tremendous success, no doubt; but he'd be the first to admit that 'something is missing'. Part of what made things work when they were small had been lost in the translation to a bigger company. No one noticed it at the time, but looking back now they see that there's no longer any organic communication and sharing, no natural collaboration and innovation. The staff is like a bunch of polite strangers working together.

How do cultures get like this?

It happens when misaligned behaviours are accepted and normalised. And it happens when new structures, rituals and artefacts are introduced without due consideration for their influence on the motivational dynamics at play.

In the next section, we'll look at some of the ways you can craft and tweak the game elements that influence behaviour and shape culture. The approach we take in this is always the same. We start with a good strategy, and then we find, test and validate the game-changing element through experimentation and play. It's 20 per cent design, and 80 per cent iteration.

Shifting dynamics

In my experience, when most people think about incorporating game design into work they usually think only in terms of enhancing competition. Adding points and leaderboards in work to rank different teams, and using 'prizes' to motivate their staff. This works — in the right context — but we need to know what type of motivational dynamic we want to bring about.

Broadly speaking, there are two main types of motivational dynamics at work: competitive and collaborative. These motivational dynamics are influenced by the game elements at play: the goals, rules and feedback.

The key is combining the right ingredients to bring about the most conducive motivational dynamics for whatever phase of work you are in.

Let's have a look at each in more detail.

Winning with competition

So you actually want to make things more competitive? Awesome. But let's darn well make sure we get this right. Because, as we know, a well-intended reward, goal or competition can seriously screw up the motivation inherent within an activity, and the collaborative dynamics within a team. Why? Because any competition involves a judgement about what constitutes winning, and what doesn't. It's the striving to gain or win something by defeating, or establishing superiority over, others.

But here's how we can ensure competition works. Most of this is about establishing clear boundaries and context for contest.

Competing against yourself

If you're competing against yourself, you're simply engaged in constructive discontent between your current personal best and your future personal best. This is good — it's progress towards mastery. It's how Olympians train, by benchmarking their score and working to get better by increments.

The negative consequences of competition are mitigated because the only party to not win in this game is your past self. And they don't mind — they're happy for you.

Competitive striving as a team

Similar to competing against yourself, competitive striving using backward comparison works. You might have a competitive dynamic with a sales team to double last year's sales. At this level, competition is clean, because it is anchored to progress. It's only when we add in further factors like performance-based incentives and contingent rewards that we enter tricky territory.

Competition within context

Sports games work to inspire fierce competition between teams — but the best players know when the game is on, and when it's off. I used to think sports like boxing were simply barbaric thuggery, until my very intelligent friend took up the sport and explained the deeper strategies of it to me. When you watch good sportsmen, they'll not hold back *anything* while the game is on. 'Go hard or go home', they say.

But here's the thing: once the finite game finishes, the person who was pummeling you in the head will be the first to give you a handshake or a hug in respect and affection.

This fierce competition works when we have clear *boundaries*. Distinct contexts between different elements of work. Just as 'what happens on the field, stays on the field', what happens within one fiercely competitive context should not bleed out into other contexts.

Fight your way to victory

A healthy team is one that is able to 'duke it out' ferociously over ideas without 'crossing the line'. The line is the boundary of the game, contained by the rules. We ensure things don't spill over the boundary—there are no personal attacks. So, if you were to facilitate an ideation session, a team of individuals passionately fighting for the best ideas is much better than a team meekly moving along with groupthink in order to not offend.

Likewise, competition works when it inspires everyone to better themselves, and when the rewards are secondary. If you are using rewards, the less tangible and more meaningful they are, the better.

My mother is an occupational health management expert and has played a big part in mine-site rescue training across various mining companies in Australia. Each year, the rescue teams from each major mine site engage in a 'Mines Rescue' competition. This involves a number of realistic scenarios, like rescuing a fallen worker from toxic gas inhalation in a dark and confined space, or diagnosing and applying emergency first aid and stabilisation to an electrocuted worker from an elevated position (while an electrical fire still burns). Incredibly complex and very realistically portrayed scenarios with Hollywood-level makeup effects ensure suspended disbelief.

These teams apply themselves to the point of exhaustion, all under the eyes of experienced referees who score and compare their performances. The rewards in this competition (a trophy, recognition, pseudo-status, a special t-shirt) are *secondary* to the experience of it. And while the competition is fierce between teams, the boundaries are clear—when the game is over, everyone knows that they are fighting for something bigger than a trophy. They're competing to improve their skills, *so they are better able to save lives when it counts.*

Now let's look at the flip side to competition—collaboration.

Taking the 'labor' out of collaboration

Collaboration simply means working with others to achieve or produce something. If you're looking to enhance collaboration, I'd say you don't need to invest in the creation of some fancy overt new game to do it.

Instead, you've simply got to *make it easier* to collaborate within the existing game. And there's a logical sequence we can follow to make collaboration work.

Identify the specific behaviours you want to see more of

Collaboration is a buzzword. Saying 'we need to be more collaborative' is the equivalent of saying 'we need to be more innovative' or 'we need to show real leadership'. These things mean different things to different people, which in effect renders them rather useless as concepts to work with.

So the first thing we'll want to identify is the *specific* types of behaviours we want to see more of. And to do that we'll need to use behaviour-based language, referring only to things that can be directly observed and measured.

'More communication' isn't a behaviour. 'Updating sales pipeline with new updates on the day they occur' or 'ensuring regional counterparts are included in project discussions' are examples of more specific behaviours. To do collaboration right, you'll want your team to establish a list of the specific behaviours that underpin collaboration—the things you want to see more of.

This activity on its own is a very good way to enhance the shared understanding and functionality of a team. It's also critically important for any executive team wanting to translate strategy into the behaviours that make it happen.

Map out the pathways

Once you've mapped out the desired behaviours you want to see more of, you've created a gap: constructive discontent between staff and the desired behaviours you want to see them engage in.

The next thing you'll want to understand is: what gets in the way of this behaviour?

Most people want to collaborate and do good work. But then stuff gets in the way, and it gets harder to engage in collaborative behaviours. Your job is to find out where this friction is.

To do this, think of six to 12 examples of staff characters, ranging across a variety of functions—a mid-level sales exec based in China, a junior HR professional in Singapore, a senior engineer from India, another sales exec from Sydney, the marketing rep from Melbourne (to use a multinational example)—whatever might typically represent the kinds of people you're looking to get 'more collaboration' from. Keep it small and relevant to start with.

Next, focus in on each character. Think about their world, then think about their pathway to engaging in a specific behaviour. What gets in the way?

I remember running this workshop with one client who wanted to see his regional executives communicate more regularly, instead of waiting for official meetings. When we ran through this activity, mapping out the pathways of representative characters, it was revealed that the executives couldn't simply arrange a conference call at short notice. It needed to be logged into the system 24 hours in advance. And, other than email (a channel that was already clogged up), they had no other platform for communicating easily. So it was no wonder things got put off until official meetings, hobbling organic collaboration. The intent was there, but the friction outweighed it.

Which brings us to our next step.

Make it super-easy to collaborate

The previous activity, pathway mapping, is a good precursor to a solid team-based workshop. It lets us know where the friction is, so we can better remove or manage it.

Sometimes friction exists because there is a lack of any alternative structure. And so it can be worthwhile exploring collaborative project-management platforms that have been designed to reduce friction. There are some very good ones available. You can even use free browser-based videoconferencing tech. Incorporate your IT staff and/or CIO if you have to, but rally together to deal creatively and constructively with the friction that lies between your people and more collaborative behaviours.

It makes sense to collaborate on the challenge of making collaboration easier.

But sometimes it's not simply a case of removing the friction at work, redesigning processes or investing in frictionless communication platforms. Sometimes you need to create space *outside* of the usual system to really ramp up collaboration.

If in doubt, hack it up

In chapter 5, when we were discussing rules, I mentioned that sometimes you need to create a productive space outside of the normal rules. Software companies are quite popular for arranging *hackathons* to enable intense collaboration. These are usually conducted with diverse teams and run over a very tight period of time — usually in the order of 24 to 72 hours. Here, nearly all barriers to collaboration are removed, and people are free to solve challenges collaboratively.

It requires a clear challenge and expert facilitation and support to pull off effectively, but the volume of collaborative work achieved in three days of intense, frictionless collaborative work could easily outweigh that of a 30-day period of work under normal conditions.

By now you can see; it's all about changing the game.

 # CHAPTER SUMMARY

This chapter unpacked some very important elements for driving progress and culture change within organisations.

First we looked at the distinction between missions and quests, and how these influence the context of our work.

Then we unpacked the importance of rituals tied to progress, looking specifically at the role of meetings. Then we explored artefacts — the tangible tokens of culture, and the relics of good work done.

With structures, rituals and artefacts covered, we then unpacked the concept of contextual momentum. Here, we calibrate the level of specificity in our approach based upon time frames, and how close or far away our goal is. This model parallels the game changer model, and sets us up to shape culture.

Culture, of course, is tackled at a behavioural and motivational level. We need to nurture and support behaviours congruent to strategy, which means developing environments that support the right motivational dynamics.

Here's how we get competition right:

- *Make the game overt.* Make sure everyone knows it's a finite game, and be sure the goals and rules are agreed upon clearly with no ambiguity. There needs to be no secret competitions, tricky new rules or hidden conditions. Give people the confidence to compete without being concerned about complications or implications.

- *Set clear and firm boundaries.* Make it clear when the game is on, and when it's over. This will help keep activities in context, so that fierce competition doesn't contaminate other, more collaborative work.

- *Contextualise it into a bigger purpose.* If you're looking to craft a competitive dynamic, make sure it clearly sits within (and contributes to) a bigger, more meaningful context. ('We're sprinting ahead to get this product launched, so we can be first to market.')

- *Go easy on rewards.* The rewards need to be secondary and understated when compared with the progress and mastery inherent to a competition or competitive play. Overemphasising rewards can discount the effort invested in triumphing, and enhance the schism between winners and 'losers'.

And here's how we nurture and support collaboration:

- *Identify the desired behaviours.* Collaboration is too conceptual to measure and change — identify specific behaviours instead.

- *Diagnose the friction.* Map out what blocks the way between people and collaborative behaviours.

- *Collaborate on collaboration.* Once you know what the challenges and obstacles are, collectively devise creative and constructive solutions.

- *Seize opportunities for intense collaboration.* In addition to everyday efforts to support collaboration, find opportunities to bring people together to undertake intense collaborative work.

By now you can see the approach we take in all of this — it's not about trying to change attitudes or beliefs, or simply defaulting to goals and rewards. Rather, we look at the gap between where things are and where we want them to be. Then we roll up our sleeves and start working pragmatically, conducting experiments and working on *the work itself,* to find the game changer.

YOU, THE GAME CHANGER

It's not worth doing something unless someone, somewhere,
would much rather you weren't doing it.

—Terry Pratchett

Huzzah! You've made it to the end, and now it's likely you'll never be able to see work, motivation and change the same way again.

No longer are progress and change dependent upon the mastery of an obscure motivational folklore, nor are they as easy to influence as simply setting a goal or incentivising a behaviour. No, no... the world of work is much more malleable.

To fix motivation, we fix the work. And we do that by tweaking, changing and playing with the goals, rules and feedback of the games at play. Through deliberate experimentation and research, we may stumble across the game changer; that newly introduced element that changes things in a significantly good way.

But to find the game changer, and to work against the friction and inherent inertia of organisations, takes grit and creative perseverance. You'll need to embark upon a hero's journey.

An epic quest...

In 1949 Joseph Campbell published a book called *The Hero with a Thousand Faces*. This book described the *monomyth* of 'The Hero's Journey', the plot structure that underpins many cultures' most prominent myths and stories. Indeed, the same structure is used in many Hollywood films today.

Here's my bastardised summary of Campbell's work (I've emphasised some of the key elements).

> The hero lives in the *ordinary world*,[1] doing ordinary things and surrounded by ordinary people. There is a *call to adventure*[2] — a chance to do something different, for a greater good. But the hero is reluctant and *refuses the call*.[3]

> But then, lo and behold! *A mentor arrives or a catalysing event*[4] occurs, whereby the hero is encouraged to *cross the first threshold*[5] and enter *a special new world*.[6] Here, they encounter many *trials, tests and tribulations*.[7]

> They persist throughout the trials, reaching their *innermost cave*[8] and cross the second threshold to *confront their demons*.[9] They *endure the ordeal*,[10] triumphing, to take possession of their *reward*.[11]

They are then pursued on *the road back*[12] to the ordinary world. But the hero is changed, and triumphs over the pursuers, crossing *the third threshold*.[13] The hero finally *returns with the elixir*,[14] a boon for the ordinary world.

Notes:

1 The hero is a normal person working within the status quo.

2 They get the call to adventure — the aspiration to do something better.*

3 But this time the resistance wins.*

4 But then something happens, and change is activated.*

5 And so they begin to explore what might be possible, conducting the first of many experiments.

6 And now they are on the path — constructive discontent has them in its grip, and they cannot simply settle.

7 But the journey is tough, and there are a lot of setbacks and disproven hypotheses.

8 Things get dark, and our hero succumbs to self-sabotage.

9 But ahoy! They lift their game and triumph.

10 They continue to endure the ordeal, staying agile and creatively committed to progress.

11 Eventually, after much experimentation, they stumble across the breakthrough game changer — the element that will make all the difference.

12 But the resistance is still there: a final gatekeeper blocks the path to progress.

13 But this time our hero has the weight of evidence and reason on their side, having changed the game so effectively that nothing can bar the way to progress.

14 And then things settle. The hero is back in the ordinary world surrounded by ordinary people doing ordinary things. And yet they are changed. They see the world differently — they see the many finite games at play, and know that they can ascend through the layers to change the game at any time.

*See figure 3.2 (p. 50).

So, in other words, this is you. You're on the hero's journey. You can refuse the call to adventure—but it's there. And there's no avoiding the fact that meaningful progress and change will take work. You will be tested.

But, with the right strategy and approach to motivation, you'll have the power to change the game—to shift behaviour, shape culture and make progress happen.

And so now, tally ho! We've got a whole world to liberate from poorly designed work.

It's time to change the game.

Onwards!

INDEX

Game over? Nay — game on!

Thank you for investing your time into this book. I hope it was of some assistance to your current mission or quest.

Now here's a funny quirk of the publishing game — by the time you read this, I may well have moved on to bigger, bolder and slightly more accurate ideas. It's part and parcel of the whole constructive discontent, constant change and progress stuff we talked about. It's science, and the everquest.

And so therefore I maintain a fairly active and rather useful 'museletter'. It's where I share the latest musings and insight in motivation strategy and gameful design. You can subscribe for free on my website » www.drjasonfox.com (there may be a small surprise)

Also, do send me an email if you feel inclined. I might be a tad slow to get back to you, but I'd love to hear about your progress-making adventures and experiments in liberating the world from poorly designed work.

I speak and consult on this stuff globally, so let me know if you'd like a hand making clever happen in your organisation.

Learn more at
www.drjasonfox.com
and say hello@drjasonfox.com

Learn more with practical advice from our experts

The New Rules of Management
Peter Cook

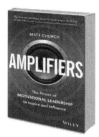

Amplifiers
Matt Church

Dealing with the Tough Stuff
Darren Hill, Alison Hill and Dr Sean Richardson

The One Thing to Win at the Game of Business
Creel Price

Digilogue
Anders Sörman-Nilsson

Bounce Forward
Sam Cawthorn

Hooked
Gabrielle Dolan and Yamini Naidu

Start with Hello
Linda Coles

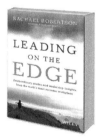

Leading on the Edge
Rachael Robertson

Available in print and e-book formats **WILEY**